FINDING MISTER/MISS RIGHT NOW?!

BY

JACK BENZA

Finding Mister/Miss Right Now?!
Copyright ©2020 Jack Benza

ISBN 978-1506-909-12-7 PBK
ISBN 978-1506-909-13-4 EBK

May 2020

Published and Distributed by
First Edition Design Publishing, Inc.
P.O. Box 17646, Sarasota, FL 34276-3217
www.firsteditiondesignpublishing.com

ALL RIGHTS RESERVED. No part of this book publication may be reproduced, stored in a retrieval system, or transmitted in any form or by any means — electronic, mechanical, photo-copy, recording, or any other — except brief quotation in reviews, without the prior permission of the author or publisher.

Although the author and publisher have made every effort to ensure that the information in this book was correct at press time, the author and publisher do not assume and hereby disclaim any liability to any party for any loss, damage, or disruption caused by errors or omissions, whether such errors or omissions result from negligence, accident, or any other cause.

Table of Contents

What's This Book About?..1

Chapter One: Operation Reboot..4
Chapter Two: The Grocery List..8
Chapter Three: Deal Breakers..12
Chapter Four: The Alternate Road..16
Chapter Five: Catfish Hunter...20
Chapter Six: Strike A Pose..24
Chapter Seven: The Bio..28
Chapter Eight: Love Me Tinder...32
Chapter Nine: Going To The Zoosk..37
Chapter Ten: Bumble Fuck!...44
Chapter Eleven: Giving The Dog A Bone..................................54
Chapter Twelve: Hinge On...59
Chapter Thirteen: Go Fish..63
Chapter Fourteen: Regular Or Decaf..75
Chapter Fifteen: Ok Stupid..79
Chapter Sixteen: Snooty Booty..84
Chapter Seventeen: Fatal Attraction...87
Chapter Eighteen: Got A Match?..90
Chapter Nineteen: Living In Perfect Harmony........................95
Chapter Twenty: The Daily Grind..100
Chapter Twenty-One: You Got To Have Faith?......................104
Chapter Twenty-Two: You Down With Oap?........................111
Chapter Twenty-Three: The Water Cooler..............................114
Chapter Twenty-Four: The First Impression..........................120
Chapter Twenty-Five: Ducks In A Row...................................126
Chapter Twenty-Six: The Hamster Wheel...............................132
Chapter Twenty-Seven: Apples To Oranges...........................136
Chapter Twenty-Eight: Covid-19 Dating 101.........................141
Epilogue..145

WHAT'S THIS BOOK ABOUT?

In 2020 more people are online dating to look for a life partner or a simple hookup. While swiping away, it is easy to have fun, get lost, overwhelmed, or even betrayed. Most people don't know where to start and lose money in the process. But then I came up with a plan to create real profiles and join the top dating websites/apps known on the world wide web. What they were known for, how much they cost, what to be aware of and how to use them.

From the process of signing up for each website/app, filling out the proper paperwork, setting up an online profile and following the proper etiquette for each dating site, I began to see what works for certain people and what doesn't. Before you start these sites, I recommend creating a Grocery List of what you want. Also, a Deal Breaker List of what you don't want.

Now I am painting this picture for everyone. My journey will consist of my stories plus the stories of my collection of peers who have lived the online dating world. Yes, they will all remain anonymous, but their stories won't. There will a range of stories from hooking up to monumental failures. Using social media to your advantage so you don't have to do these sites. From fake online profiles with fake information and pictures that doesn't look like the person in the picture. People that lost a significant other and found love later. To catfishing where you think you are talking to one person and you are talking to someone else.

This book is for everyone. From people looking for love, a hookup, some one that just got divorced and must get back out there and even people that are married and are just curious what it's like to be out there again. This is that book. Where do you start? What do you say? Which website do I pick? For example, don't pick Tinder if you want a life partner. We are going to cover all of this. For the record this book will mention any shortcoming these website/apps may have.

Make yourself a goal before you start. What do I want? What am I entitled to? What will I not allow or tolerate? So, when we talk about the process of signing up with these websites and setting up your online profile you will be more honest with yourself and you will realize it's a lot easier knowing what you want.

Dating is like having a full-time job. You have a certain behavior when you're doing your job. There are certain expectations you hope to reach while pursuing your career and in turn there are certain things your boss expects from you and your job performance. Every new date for me is like my first day on the job. I must look my best and make a good first impression, so I earn a second day on the job. But sometimes you find out some jobs are awful, a lot of work and you ask yourself, "Why am I at this job?". The second date is the second interview. You already know what you need to from the first date, but you may be on the fence with certain issues. The stakes are now higher.

Finding Mister/Miss Right Now will examine the feelings that are now coming up and it will flat out define your mission. I want to start a family. I want all the things that my friend has, because why I can't I have that too?! Well maybe a part of you feels that I have nothing to offer someone. Another part of you feels how can anyone deal with my stuff and in turn how can I deal with their stuff? Time to get out of your head and lose that way of thinking. Time to come up with a new way of thinking and this time do it right. Give yourself an honest shot. At least try and if you die alone and it doesn't work out for you, then there is no regret.

When I started, I knew things were going to be different. I was on a mission and I knew I was going to have to go to a place that honestly scared the shit out of me, The online dating world. I knew she was out there, and I was going to have to find her. Even if I didn't, I was going to fucking try! Maybe she was in a place I never went. That is the online dating world. It is the undiscovered country. But like me and many of my peers I was ready to set sail and I would take the necessary preparations to do this. To face this. To experience this. Yes, it will be some work, but there will be some reward too. Trust us.

No, we are not guaranteeing you will meet someone. That is not our mission. Our mission is to take you on the journey. Let's sign up for all the sites in no particular order. Match, eHarmony, Zoosk, Tinder, Bumble, Plenty of Fish, Elite Singles, Hinge, Our Time, Christian Mingle, Ashley Madison, Jdate, Okcupid, Grindr, Coffee Meets Bagel, and more random websites that you probably never heard of. But we all are moving in the same direction.

Billy Crystal said in Harry Met Sally during the New Year's Eve scene, "When you meet somebody you want to spend the rest of your life with, you want the rest of your life to start as soon as possible.". Now that message is solid and resonates in your heart. You deserve an honest shot at this. I'm going to break it down for you. In the end you will be in "the know". Ready?! Let's get started.

CHAPTER ONE

OPERATION REBOOT

This chapter is about changing your way of thinking when it comes to online dating and I am using myself as the prime example. I have hurt myself for years thinking I wasn't good enough for women I would consider a girlfriend. Now I will go up to any woman and start a conversation with her. But when it comes to women, I would consider a possible life relationship with, way different story. To be honest I am not the best with money. I love spending money on women, going out and treating myself to the best stuff. Great, but not if I want to start a family so that had to change.

So, I had to reprogram myself in a lot of ways to get to the right mindset for my mission. There were five beliefs I had in my head that prevented me from starting a relationship. Here they are:

1. I have no money to pursue this type of endeavor.

2. My career is more important to me. (Acting)

3. I don't have time to hang out. Love my days off.

4. I love dating whoever I want. (Freedom)

5. How is she going to deal with me? I'm a handful.

It is expensive to date and if you're the guy it is even worse. More people are going Dutch these days and some dating sites request it for first time daters. But most men want to win over the women and honestly most women want to be won over. So, what does this mean for the guy? He must put dating in his monthly bills like cable, rent and a car payment. Maybe to fit dating in your budget you must give up cable. I did for nine months and it was one of the worst decisions of my life. I didn't have TV. I had seen everything on Netflix and the only thing I had to show for those nine months of dating was 6 fun memories. I needed to be smarter with money. Mind reset. How? "Cheap Dates".

Cheap dates save you money and honestly open more conversation than an expensive dinner date. What is a cheap date without making yourself look cheap? Here is a group suggestion. Now did this strategy work? Yes. Numerous times and was quite effective.

1. Coffee. Simple. Does not involve alcohol. Can happen at any time of day. Maybe throw in a muffin.

2. A hike. Exercise. Getting out there. Watching each other sweat. Plenty of time for conversation and get information.

3. Netflix. When you are building a relationship, online interests come up. TV shows are one of them. If there is a TV show you folks have in common make it a date. Plus, things happen when the bedroom is ten feet away.

4. Picnic and movie. There are places like parks that show movies and you can bring food. Great way to show off your chef skills.

5. Standup comedy. You laugh. Two drink minimum. People love to laugh.

Career. I came out to Hollywood to act. That was my priority. If a woman I date isn't digging that then it is not going to happen. You must make decisions that affect both of you. She may not like my job. She may not give a shit if she believes in me. There are people like that and there are materialistic people that want security. I was going to think differently. She may like my commercials. She may not care you if you are bringing money home. Mind reset. Give her a chance to make that decision.

Time. I work forty hours a week at a restaurant when I am not acting. Five hours a week working out. Ten hours a week acting. Point is how do I have time to hang out with somebody else? I love my days off. Question is what am I really doing on my days off that couldn't include somebody else? I like drinking on my Sundays off and watching TV. But why can't someone be next to me watching it. Mind reset. Spend my time more wisely by making time for them.

Freedom. Dating who I want, and when I want. I mean the single guy has it all. Can leave whenever he wants. The single life is lonely also. Yes, there is a freedom, but like anything else it can get tired. What I have learned is people that talk about their freedom run away from commitment. They are afraid to take that dive into the water of dating. That has been me for years. Mind reset. Open my heart to a commitment.

How is she going to deal with me? When I drink, I snore. I'm kind of fat. I have two dogs that like to pee a lot. I like to get up and dance. I'm the animated Italian New Yorker. I may be too much. Sound familiar? I mean do you think like this? Like you are not good enough. I do. Most of my friends do. It's a mind fuck. As I said in the beginning what do I have to offer anyone? Stop. Stop immediately. Mind reset. No more assuming anything. You don't know what she will like or hate. Let her be the judge of that.

Ok let's do this. Now I had a new way of thinking. A clean slate. Forget my past relationships or tragedies or even great loves. Now I was taking a trip with no expectations. It was a kind of freedom. From my peers these are three things that helped.

1. Positive thinking. I always thought it can happen. It is going to happen.

2. Day Dreaming. I daydreamed myself meeting someone.

3. Talking about it. Talk to other people about what you want.

I was changing my way of thinking. How I viewed a potential date and how I would act. So, I came up with a simple wish list first. What do I want? That became my Grocery List and now it was time to shop.

CHAPTER TWO

THE GROCERY LIST

Every dater should have a list of what they want. I call it the Grocery List. Like when you go shopping you make a list of things you want to enjoy. Same thing here, but let's be more specific when we are talking dating. Here is a compiled top twenty list of the most common things daters want to know about their significant others.

1. Looks. Yeah, they kind of matter.

2. Career. Do they have a good job?

3. Age. Are they young? Can they have kids? What is the maturity level here?

4. Pet lover? Are they a dog person? Cat person? Or any pets at all?

5. Kids? Do they like kids? Would they want kids?

6. Alcohol. Does this person like to drink with me?

7. Do you take care of yourself? Completely different from looks. Do these people exercise. I want someone in shape.

8. Nutrition. Is there something you don't eat? Because dating a Vegan or someone who doesn't eat what I eat can be a major turnoff.

9. Drugs? Do they partake? If so which ones?

10. Smoking. Do you smoke or not?

11. Education. Does this person have a degree?

12. Health issues. Some people might not want to deal with sick people.

13. Debt. Most people don't want to deal with other's debt.

14. Relationships. Is there an ex or baby daddy or momma I don't know about?

15. Religion. What do you believe in?

16. Race. Is there a race you wouldn't date?

17. Family. What was the upbringing like?

18. Friends. Does this person have friends?

19. Background check. Does this person have a history? There are ways to check this.

20. Transportation. Do you drive?

Now this just a list of the most popular things that come up and believe me there is more, but you get the gist. Make your Grocery List. You deserve the best and you need to be specific. Know what you want. Now this list may change once you get to know the person and you will compromise. Here's a huge dating hint…everyone has luggage and you are going to have to compromise this list many times if you like the person. When making your profile everyone exaggerates and lies at times.

But the list is your floor plan. You can't go blind into this. You may have to lie and exaggerate too. Time is something a lot of people don't have, and they don't want to waste it. They get disappointed. So, don't waste each other's time. Yes, people lie but on things like age, how much they make and their habits. But if you drink everyday some people may not want to deal with that. Drugs as well. Every site will ask you. Do you drink once a day, not or just socially? That word socially is a trick, but some people think four drinks is normal while others may see it as an alcoholic. We will work on our profiles later depending on the websites we talk about and that answer will vary and change, but for now stick with a solid answer.

Your Grocery List is your backbone throughout this entire process and next chapter our Deal Breaker List will be our beliefs and credibility. Again, be honest to a point during this process for yourself. There may be someone out there for you. This is your plan and you will build an online profile that will define you. Don't write something that will embarrass you later. News flash. When you are done with a website, they pass your info onto sex websites that will bug the shit out of you when you start getting emails from these sites. Most of it ends up on your spam. Match, Zoosk and eHarmony as respected as they are were my first websites I was on and only they had my information. How did this happen? When you cancel your membership, they don't care about you anymore. My name, email and all the info I shared is not important to them anymore. They may deny this, but I have the emails to prove it.

Remember what you write on the internet stays on the internet and can be used against you. Every picture, quote and profile lives forever. It doesn't die when you cancel your membership. There are some bitter bitches out there. Some people troll this shit and use it against you later. But my advice is having your Grocery List and put it out there with a safeguard knowing there are people out there with their own agenda.

Some people may just want to fuck you and call you a conquest even though you want something else. Then temporarily you may revise your list knowing some of these pitfalls. Or they may really like you readjust and make it more precise.

Here are my top revisions:

1. Thirty-five-year-old woman that can have a kid.

2. Looks. Semi attractive OK. I would deal.

3. I would like to settle down soon as possible.

4. They must have a career and contribute.

5. Habits should be something I can deal with.

6. I want someone with minimal luggage. Pets and kids.

Kind of like having a shorter Grocery List I knew what I was looking for. So, I started looking at it frequently when I went through profiles. I developed a pattern for looking at profiles that worked for me and started setting up dates. I was just starting to think like a dater. Like somebody that was hungry I wanted to eat. I now knew what I wanted. This was just a strategy and that is what you need if you are going to invest time into this endeavor. I will admit I was scared. What if this new strategy doesn't work? I'm sure there will be some roadblocks along the way, but if I can get around them then maybe I would find her.

CHAPTER THREE

DEAL BREAKERS

What are the things in your life that you can't allow and how important are they to you? Time to make your Deal Breaker List which is things you won't deal with when it comes to finding a partner. Once you make that list go over it one more time to see how important it is to you. Can you compromise with your new partner and take it off your list?

This was my list.

1. They must like kids.
2. They must want kids.
3. They must like dogs.

4. I wanted a Caucasian woman either Italian or Hispanic.

5. I wanted a Catholic Woman.

6. I didn't want a woman with kids. I didn't want to raise someone else's kids.

7. I didn't want someone who smokes.

8. I didn't want a materialistic woman who was all about money.

9. I didn't want someone who does drugs.

10. I didn't want someone who was divorced. To me that was damaged goods with luggage.

Now I know that some of you are thinking wow that is a picky list. But this is my list and I am entitled to it. Just as you are yours. But most people think this way and they can only live a certain way. But that is what compromise is all about. When I meet somebody there are certain things I can't stand about a person and I'm sure there are certain things they can't stand about me. But if there is an attraction you learn to deal with some of those things until you get to your Deal Breaker List. Then it gets real. Remember the Vegan. Notice that is not on my Deal Breaker List, but it was one of the things that bugged me about her. I just never ate meat in front of her. I was falling in love with her. She didn't want to have kids and I did. I tried to persuade her into it, but her Deal Breaker List had no kids. Again, nothing wrong with that. But that is a number two thing for me and I'm not changing that.

Same goes for my top five. Hard to work around that. In my list one and two pretty much work together. But it doesn't mean I am going to find a woman who likes both. They can like kids, but not want to have them. So, when I am finding out information on them during our date I would first ask if they like them. If they do,

I eventually move on to the next question. But asking a woman if they want kids must be more subtle and specific. Some may want to adopt and again I want my blood in that kid and not someone else's. So, adoption is kind of on my Deal Breaker List. They must want kids means me and you starting a family. It is a heavy question, but one that must be asked if you want to move forward. They must like dogs, because I have two. Now if they have dogs, our dogs must get along. If they don't this partnership isn't going to work. If they do then eventually, we must get a bigger place. Ask any dog owner and most of the time their dog comes first. That is their children. Same goes for me. I want a Caucasian woman who is either Italian or Hispanic, because that is how I grew up. I want that upbringing for my family. Now I have dated all different type of races and this is what I prefer for my wife. Now if I meet someone who is not this and wants to start a family and I am really attracted to them, then I may have to make a consideration. Again, this Deal Breaker List is not set in stone, but it must be part of your thought process. Same goes for my number five I want a Catholic woman but doesn't mean I am going to get it. I have dated several Jewish women one of which stole my heart. However, I would prefer a Catholic wedding and upbringing.

So, once I had a new way of thinking I had to come up with my solid list of Deal Breakers. This is extremely important for two reasons. One is Time and the other is Money. I knew my window was closing for starting a family, so I had to be strict on my deal breakers. For example, my top three deal breakers are they must like kids, be able to have kids, and like dogs. Now some people may be thinking that is a shitty way of thinking, but I knew what I wanted, and I didn't want to waste time. I usually would find out this information within the two dates, but keep in mind a lot of people lie when it comes to their online profiles.

With that information the other reason we have deal breakers is money. I didn't want to spend money on someone that wasn't part of my mission. So, I would learn in time to go on cheap dates. Again, these were dates that I set up so I can read her behavior and save money at the same time. If I had a coupon, I would use it on purpose just to see her reaction. At times I would get a wow that is kind of cheap reaction to which I would respond with a don't worry you're not paying for its reaction.

Deal breakers can be a bitch but are a necessity for what you want. You don't want to be trapped or waste anyone's time. People have different agendas. The Vegan had a different agenda and I must respect that even if I had feelings for her. She did me a favor. Most of the stories you will experience in this book is about sacrifice and seeing that making hard choices is necessary. Some of this for you may sound like commonsense. But for people that want the big picture we are building a foundation and now we are going to take a journey towards the online dating world. But first let's a make a slight detour.

CHAPTER FOUR

THE ALTERNATE ROAD

Before I started my online dating mission, I wanted to explore the social media route which is the red head stepchild of online dating. Instagram, Facebook, and Snapchat are online platforms where dating and meeting someone is so easy. I had known most of these people at some point in my life and their whole online history was right there. I could tell who was single and where they were hanging out. So, I hit up everyone I thought would help me with my mission. One of which was the 32-year-old lady that I had a history with, who I'll call Bella. Bella wanted to co-parent with me, which is raise a kid together, but not have a relationship. We hung out several times and really talked about it. However, after dating a while we realized it wouldn't be fair to the kid we were going to raise.

Another one of my friends fell in love with a semi famous girl that did stand up. He knew her material, where she was going to perform and what she was going to talk about. How? Because she posted it on Facebook, Instagram, and Snapchat. Now did this girl want the attention? Probably not, but she posted it on all these websites and probably not knowing invited this guy and other guys with the same agenda. Was she asking for this? I mean she had over 1000 likes and views. Yeah maybe she did want this attention. My friend eventually did date her. Didn't end well, but for three months they posted everything they did together. My friend obtained the goal of being with her, which was all he really wanted in the first place.

Now what I am suggesting you do before you delve into the world of online dating is become a detective and see if there is anybody out there that you overlooked? Or does anyone of your friends have a friend you may be interested in? If there is then start following them online or even start liking some of the things they post. Eventually over time you may comment on something they like. They may comment back. Now you're starting a conversation. Zoosk is a dating website that specializes in just texting each other with messages that I will touch on later. This is very similar to what you are doing. You are building a relationship. Now this person you started the conversation with may ask their friends about you if they are interested. However, they may ask their friends who the hell is this guy he is stalking me. Now is this stalking? Yeah kind of, but if you are posting something and make it public, then you are inviting people to comment. Hey worst case scenario they block you.

But if there is a connection you can instant messenger that person and that is very similar to online dating. People who have Facebook and Instagram accounts mention if they are single. Believe me nine out of ten are looking and putting out that bait for that special someone. The most popular bait is anything that shows you work out. Go on any social media platform and if you look at any single profile one of the last five posts will be that person doing some type of exercise. Which conveys I am an active person. The second most popular post is usually something with food which shows them either cooking or at a place they like to go eat. This message conveys I love to cook, and I love to eat. Take me there. The third most popular is usually them with a pet or their niece and nephew which conveys I have love to give. But the one you really must look out for is when they post anything that shows their political beliefs and religious beliefs. This one tells the story. If they are democrat, republican, atheist, feminist, or whatever. Just look at their history and that will tell you the type of person they are. Were some of their posts late at night? That could mean they are drunk or high when they post. Are they posting disturbing things during the day? You start learning their thought process.

There are however people that don't post anything incriminating or revealing. Now this is where you become the detective. Three things you do if you are interested and want the information. First you google them and see if anything comes up. Where they went to school or work. Check out images. Are there pictures of that person with their ex? See what type of person they date. Just because they don't post anything doesn't mean their ex didn't tag and post it. Nothing wrong with gathering some intel on the person you want to date and spend time with. Two is LinkedIn. Where did they work and what do they do for a living? Also, a great thing LinkedIn does is they let you see who logged into your profile history. It is like setting up a bait trap where anyone that finds you interesting is right there. The way to send the message back is check out their profile so they see that you logged into their business. Three is the old-fashioned way. Call or text a friend you have in common for a set up. Or just flat out ask them out. You will get your yes or no right there.

Social media doesn't cost you a thing and it saves you time. A lot of the dating websites will get your money and suck you in. The thing social media has that dating sites don't is information. It is all there. The history of the person. Where they eat, live, sleep, dated and worked. Dating sites, you are starting from scratch and one bad impression and you are done. You must dig for information slowly. You never know who you are talking to. Remember that. Social media has it all there for you and the conversation is loose. Online dating is a slow methodical pace that can eventually take off. Social media you can throw a crazy one liner in there that may work or bomb. Either way you can move on to the next person with their history displayed.

But the most important thing to remember about social media is it is not private like online dating. People can see your history. What you are like. Who you liked and pursued. Ahhh the realization. Once you put it out there on the internet it is out there. Some people forget this. You could have been a different person five years ago than you are now. However, someone checking you out may see the person from five years ago and that can hurt your chances. So, once you are done with social media and you realize I may need some privacy you are ready for online dating. But remember one thing. Not everybody has your agenda. There may be some people out there you may come across with their own agenda. I must talk about this in the next chapter before we hit the dating websites.

CHAPTER FIVE

CATFISH HUNTER

A catfish is someone who creates a false online identity. Very common on social media and online dating. The purpose of catfishing and why the term was created is there are people online that want to be other people and they may look at your picture and just want to be with you. You may be straight, and they may be gay, so they will create a false account that shows a picture of the opposite sex and start a conversation with you. They may be straight and want to seek revenge on you like an ex. They may just want to steal your identity. Be careful what you always say online.

Five things to remember in this situation:

1. Catfish people will use what you say to them against you.

2. This information can be used to get what they want.

3. They can blackmail you.

4. Even if they are not catfishing you remember what you say online can be used by anybody.

5. This can be really embarrassing and can scar you emotionally.

I got catfished. I thought I was talking to Brenda. A girl I met on Tinder. 35 years old. Red head. Nice body. I told her I wanted kids and she said she was into it, but shy. She told me things that got me lost in the conversation. I told her personal things. So, I planned to meet her five minutes from where I live. The intention was to take her to a restaurant or even just to my place, because of the conversations we had which were all via messaging. We were supposed to meet at The Grove in Los Angeles, a public place with lots of people. The time to meet was 6pm around dinner time. I had flowers in my hand. Ten minutes go by. Then to my right a guy that looked like someone you would see at Comic-Con, with a deuce bag swagger, comes up to me smiling and says,

"Hey Jack, I'm Brenda!"

I said, "Who the fuck are you?!"

He said, "Brenda. Yeah, I know, not what you expected. But what do you think?!

Immediately I knew what was happening and the first thought in my head was why the fuck did I use my real name?! The adrenaline came in and I got angry. I felt violated and I let this mother fucker have it. He wasn't intimidating but he was smiling.

I said, "I think I should crack your head open. Get the fuck out of here!

He said, "Hey Jack relax, why you so tense?"

I moved toward him, and he took five steps back, but started hopping. I changed my demeanor to calm and smiled instantly knowing this guy was harmless and probably got off on this.

I said, "I could call the cops."

He said, "Bye." Then took off.

I looked around to see if there was a camera or maybe the actual person Brenda that I thought I had been talking to. But everyone was walking around like nothing had happened and I didn't pursue the guy. I just went home and tried to look up the account on Tinder, but it was deleted like it never happened. The picture of Brenda gone. I reported to Tinder what had happened and they with half a heart said there is nothing we can do. They told me I could call the cops, but then I would further embarrass myself and this may make a funny story in some precinct. I let it go. I felt violated, but then after some time I laughed almost like I deserved it. I got duped and I tried to see it through the eyes of that guy. But the only image I had was him trying to please himself to my picture and things I may have told him.

So, what is the lesson here? Just because you are talking to somebody online doesn't mean it is them. Until you meet them. It could be somebody underage which happened to a friend of mine. It could be somebody else entirely with the same sex profile which happened to a friend of mine. So, don't put all your cards in one basket. Meet them first before you get personal. Now I know this may scare the shit out of you and you are like sorry Jack I'm done reading. Hold on I'm just telling you there are sharks in the water be careful. However, it is a real big ocean out there with many possibilities, so just be aware.

The mindset of a catfish is simple. Why do it? Here's a list and once you understand the motivation then you may move on from my story and jump in the water.

1. They are insecure people looking for something in their lives. So, they get off on fucking with others by any means necessary.

2. They want something from you. They are bad people that may want to pressure you into giving them money.

3. It could be someone you fucked over in a former relationship. Let's look at three for a second. My friend broke up with his girlfriend and it ended bad. So, she created a Facebook profile separate from my friend saying he finally came out of the closet. The profile name was one letter off, but friend requests were sent out and over two hundred people responded saying congrats on coming out. My friend got wind of it, reported to Facebook, and found out she created the profile. My friend had the account deleted and had to explain to over two hundred people it wasn't real. Did my friend deserve it? Probably not, but there are some vindictive people out there and online dating and social media is an easy way to get revenge. So be careful who you talk to and what you say.

Now there are some stories people have told me about being bullied and victimized. Unfortunately, those stories and people exist. There are simply people that want to have sex out there and they use online dating as their tool, and they fuck with people's emotions. Be careful. Don't meet people in shady places. If you feel uncomfortable at any time get out. Don't put yourself in a situation where you don't have control. Call the cops if something goes down. Don't be afraid.

CHAPTER SIX

STRIKE A POSE

The right picture is the first and may be the only impression you leave on your potential dater. Most websites you get six. But in the realistic dating world they only look at one. So, which one do you use? Three types stand out.

1. The Spontaneous shot where you are out on the town. So, dress your best. Have an outfit ready. Make sure if you're a guy, things are pressed. For the women your make up is perfect and you look natural. It can be where you like to hang out. Where you want to hang out. Daters look at every shot like it's a crime scene. They look at everything. The littlest thing can turn them off and you are done. For example, don't be the guy at a bar taking a selfie with hot women in the back holding a drink. Right away women think

you are not taking care of business. Why don't you ask them out? Most pictures show women with their friends in the picture and right away the dater is like which one are you? This shit happens repeatedly, and I believe the intention is they will check out my five other pictures. Wrong. There is only one chance to make an impression and let me see it.

2. The Working Out shot. OK you work out. People get intimidated by this. Most people that date want the Netflix night right away. They just want to fuck and figure things out later. Don't get me wrong a physical lifestyle is great but those are follow-up pics. Number two and three maybe. News flash everyone works out in some form. I don't want to see you sweat. Unless you have washboard abs, and this really is your lifestyle then fuck yeah, it's number one. But it really is a turnoff if you want to make a first impression. People don't want to deal with that. They may work fifty hours a week and the last thing on their mind is working out. Or taking a two-hour hike away from the bed. However, if you honor the healthy lifestyle then fucking use it. You may want to weed people out and live a happy lifestyle.

3. I have kids and I have pets' shots. Wow OK! First impression is I don't want to raise these kids. I like to sleep and no I don't want to wake up next to these animals ever. I have animals and now I must see if my animals coexist with yours. Yes, it's nice you have kids and pets. Yes, it is nice you share love with pets, but man that is a lot of luggage and this should never be photo one. More like five and six. If they like the first four pics, they will deal with five and six.

So, what is the right picture? You have your Grocery List and Deal Breaker List. It should be the one that mirrors your list. Be proud of it. Not everyone is going to like your first picture, but all it takes is one. That is what you are working for. So, if your first three is any of those three choices then own it and stick with it. The pictures you do need are ones where you are out. Proud of. Ones with family that show your habits and hobbies. Your job. If you are a construction worker show you on the job. They should be real and not fake.

Many of the profile pictures that I see are people taking a five second selfie and they look frustrated after filling out the application. These pictures look like shit. They allow you to upload photos but most of them these days must be verified, and they must be current like the website Zoosk does. They don't want people looking older than their pics. It's not fair to the dater. However, most pictures these days are something you can upload like Tinder where you don't pay and it's easier to trick daters and even catfish daters.

A great app daters are using these days is "Boomerang" that allows you take a series of pictures like it's a small video and people are adding this to their apps and making them look better than a solid picture. It just gives you a solid up in the competition compared to other daters in the dating world not using it and it doesn't cost a thing. A video over a pic is everything, Actors are using this in acting called a "Slate Shot" where it brings the headshot to life and it helps. Why not use this in dating?

You have two seconds to make the impression. If they don't like you, they swipe left on Tinder. They like they swipe right; I will hit that up later. Your pictures are your representation and they tell a story. Why not tell a story in fashion. Why not show pics that you take time to set up? Don't do the frustrated half ass shots that people do on these sites. And women please stop using bathroom shots in your profile, it is overused and mundane.

Do I want to get laid? Then show me shots where I want to fuck you. Same goes for gay people. Entice me. Invite me. Be in a position. Think about it. Most of these shots are people showing off their body in a situation. I will hit up every dating site that is relevant for your Grocery List. But man, you must be creative if you want to make an impression.

Next let's talk about your bio.

CHAPTER SEVEN

THE BIO

    You have five hundred words or less to impress your dater. So, what do you say? I mean you have your Grocery List and it should be based on that but more specific. Never use your Deal Breaker List here. It will kill you. Deal Breaker Lists are only for dates one and two that we will hit up later.

    The bio is your story that you will use on every dating site. It should be the same on every dating site you use for your intentions. For example, I want a woman I can meet and start a family with. So, my opening line should be, "I am single guy looking for a long-term relationship that can lead to starting a family." First line state your intention. Change roles. "I am a single guy looking for no strings attached, and I want to have fun." Intention is I want to get laid with no luggage. People don't usually read more after that. If they like your picture and that line that's all you need in the dating world.

But some people want more. What do you do for a living? Do you have any luggage? Kids? Pets? Exes? So how do you word it? I mean pictures usually tell a story, but most people like to hide shit. Your bio is your explanation. Don't tell them any of that shit in your bio. Instead set the bait and lure them in. Make them want to contact you and get that intel. The second thing you say is a great fucking thing about you. Something they would tell their friends or anyone at work. This info is based on your job or your hobbies or made up bullshit that makes them strike a chord and be into you. True or not. You want them saying I am dating this guy because…

Top five best answers:

1. I love to donate to cancer, because my family member survived it.
2. I have run eight marathons, because I love to challenge myself.
3. I am looking for somebody that wants a best friend in a life partner.
4. I want to love somebody that puts me first.
5. I want somebody that I can take care of.

Why these five answers? This was the like on over one hundred people's profiles when I went undercover on ALL THESE WEBSITES. People immediately donated, talked about a huge physical achievement, wanted a friend, wanted to be taken care of or wanted to take care of somebody. All bullshit! All made up stories. Maybe some real but after some digging bullshit. So, what do you write?

Go with the flow I mean if everybody is lying or exaggerating. Why not you? Tell them any of these five. Remember the date is where you find the truth. But until then you must get the date so play the game. Lie your ass off. Blow smoke up the internet's ass.

Another thing that gets people is hard ass truth! Say something about yourself that is true, but with a dig. Standup comedy is funny when the standup comic makes fun of themself in a situation that relates to people. So, find that truth. Share that situation and take the dive. For example, I usually date Catholic women, but I never get a word in, because they are telling me all about themselves. But I'm a listener. Message I date Catholic women and there is a funny side to me. Be clever.

Most importantly what do you like to do. Travel. Go out and eat. Karaoke. Give this person an idea where to take you out. Be honest. They want to impress you. So, give them a hint. They won't take you to a bar if you don't drink. Common sense there. If your ass likes hiking, then mention it.

Your Five hundred words let people know who you are and what you want. Don't ever be honest. But make sure your Grocery List is honored. There must be a sense of urgency without the desperation factor in there. Remember you have all the time in the dating world, but you don't. Your fate is decided in ten seconds with a bio. People will stop reading your shit after the second sentence. Like a profile pic. So, suck them in the first four sentences. The rest just add to it.

Top four sentences that suck them in:

1. I'm looking/not looking for a long-time relationship.

2. Willing to try new things.

3. Have never done a dating site before.

4. Want to meet new people.

OK look at number one. The most common for both, but both answers can be bullshit. People looking for a relationship are also looking for a good time. Why settle when you can have fun? Also, the people not looking for anything usually find something, but are afraid to admit they are.

Number two means yeah anal, threesome, or even yachting. Very vague, but there is no interpretation. So, with what I just said all those options are on the table. You never know who you are going to meet.

Number three. Yeah, I never had a drink before. Horse shit. Don't play naïve. You are just trying to hide any guilt you felt in the past and give yourself a clean slate. You did Tinder. You did Myspace. You did some form of dating and are trying to be a born again. Don't work here.

Number four. If you want to meet new people, then what dating site did you fail at? But if that is true how far are you willing to go? Cause this world will suck you up and take advantage of you. That screams virgin. But it also screams do over.

Again, get your story in. This will be the impression to back up your pics. Some of the best bios are under one hundred words short and sweet. Some people feel they need to use all five hundred words. But bottom line three sentences can sum you up. Single looking for love. Want a family right now. No bullshit.

CHAPTER EIGHT

LOVE ME TINDER

Swipe right you like somebody. Swipe left oh hell no. Based solely on a picture, daters barrel through pictures of other potential daters in a matter of seconds. If you happen to swipe right and another dater swipes you right, then a connection is made, and contact begins. Now besides having the right picture the other two features this website uses is age on every picture and location.

Age is something that is never honestly used on this website. People outright lie about that. Age range is the proper word. When people lie about their age it is pretty much the age range they want to date. Tinder gives you the option under "Settings" to pick the age range you want. No wasting time. Of course, you can pick the men, women or everyone option. From most of the other stories I have acquired Tinder is pretty much a let's hookup now website and the best part is it is free to a point. I will hit that later.

But the other feature Tinder offers under "Discovery Settings" is "Location". How close or far away are you? From one mile away to the maximum distance of one hundred miles away you can set how far you willing to go to meet someone. As the dater you set it to five miles and then everyone within five miles of you will be at your fingertips and that information is right there under "Name" and "Age". Location is huge when it comes to meeting someone and starting a relationship. But with this website more people are looking for the quick hookup so usually five miles is the standard setting. But I do have someone I know that met someone on Tinder and they live thirty miles from each other.

More things you can add on your profile picture is your job and your education. People do want to know what you do for a living. Also does this person have an education. Next career. Most people again completely lie here for both. Daters who put down hospitality as a career are usually a bartender or a waiter. Me, for the purpose of this book and knowing my profile was fake, I said actor. I was honest about my education B.A. Rutgers University. I did though want to have fun with this, so I picked a profession no one ever picks. But I did want people to know I did have an education.

The best part is creating your profile or story you want to tell people. Of course, mine was a profile I created just to see what traffic I could get. Using my profile as an example I said I was a brash Italian New Yorker with heart. You may have seen me on TV or a reality show. Now here I also mentioned that I was looking for someone to share my life with which can kill any chance of a one-night stand. But I also did mention I am open and willing to try new things which can suck people in to believing I can pull a one-night stand with them. I did mention I wanted kids and that can scare most people away or it can even show OK he is here to find love. Finally setting up your sexual orientation is the last part of your profile and Tinder gives you the opportunity to pick up to three. The choices are Straight, Gay, Lesbian, Bisexual, Asexual, Demisexual, Pansexual, Queer and Questioning. Also, they give you the option of showing this on your profile.

Now once you set up your profile you will have the opportunity to add up to ten pictures. I put up a head shot. Me in front of the Hollywood sign with the dogs. Crossing the finish at The LA Marathon. Random pictures of me on set dressed as a cop and one as a weatherman. I wanted to create this guy who was always entertaining or in front of the camera and giving the impression that I was outgoing and maybe even famous. What kind of people would I attract? As I mentioned earlier, I did get catfished off this website. However, I did attract a lot of traffic most of which was only five miles away. Most of these dates people did not look like their picture at all. Some easy examples are they looked older, maybe heavier and some didn't bother to wear any makeup or even try. I mean I saw ten pictures of somebody I found interesting and the night of the date none of those pictures looked like her. However, I did meet some interesting people I won't lie. Many of the people I interviewed told me Tinder has the highest ratio for people that want to get laid.

Ok so now you are looking at the app and you start to see pictures of potential daters. Bottom left you see a swirling yellow arrow running counterclockwise which once you press it takes you to "Tinder Plus". Now this is where Tinder starts to charge you to increase your chances of making a match which it does.

First off Tinder Plus charges:

1. $7.50 a month for a year.

2. $11.25 a month for six months

3. $17.99 for one month.

For that you get:

1. Unlimited Likes so you can swipe until your hearts content.

2. Skip The Line" which makes you a top profile for 30 minutes in your area.

3. Limits what others see about you and you can only be shown to people you like.

4. Swipe around the world feature. Paris. NY. Sydney go.

5. Gives you 5 Super Likes a day.

Honestly the best deal here is six months. One year is too long. If you pay one month thirty days goes by fast and it really isn't enough time to give it an honest shot. If you are into someone and it takes two weeks to get to know them, then you realize it wasn't what you expected. Honestly, you really didn't have enough time to use the app to its full potential. Remember this is an investment in your time and money. If you pay a little extra you get extra and again it's your time. For $67.50 it is worth it compared to other dating sites. Plus, there are always new daters being thrown into the mix.

Next on the app is the "X Button" which has the same action as swiping "Left". When you swipe left a big nope appears and you never see them again. The "Heart Button" means you like someone, and it has the same action as swiping "Right" where you see the word "Like". You will also see a "Star Button" which is a "Super Like" and you get one a day so use them wisely. A "Lightning Bolt Symbol" means you are looking for a "Boost" which means you become a top profile in your area for thirty minutes which they call "Skip The Line". Now remember if you stay in one area this will work. You can't be in your car driving. The app bases it on your location and where your phone is.

Of course, this is where they charge:

1. 10 Boosts for $3.60 each.
2. 5 Boosts $4.50 each.
3. 1 Boost $4.99 each.

Waste of time. Save your money. This is just another feeble attempt at Tinder trying to take your money. The final attempt Tinder does to take your money is "Tinder Gold" where they charge you to see which people liked you so you can make an instant match.

1. 12 months $11.25 a month.
2. 6 Months $16.92 a month.
3. 1 Month $26.99 a month.

A friend of mine took the one month and now he had a checklist of all the woman he could sleep with. There were nine potential dates on his list, and he met seven of them. He ended up sleeping with four. So, if you are looking for a quick hookup, then hello Tinder is your app.

Again, Tinder is the type of dating app for people looking for the quick hookup. There really is no depth here. Based mostly on looking at a picture that is all you have. Again, the great thing about Tinder is the location of people. You can find love five miles away. A decision is made in two seconds, so the picture is everything. It's free. There is no difficulty with this app and to be honest swiping is fun.

CHAPTER NINE

GOING TO THE ZOOSK

This is, believe it or not the most successful dating app out there when it comes to making a connection with somebody looking for a relationship. Over forty million singles are on this dating site. It is free to browse and the best thing about this site is photos are verified, which means you get what you see. No catfishing. No people that don't look like their pictures. This is a straight in your face let's start talking app. Mostly done by texting this is how you will connect with people. So, make sure your punctuation and language are proper.

Let's start from the beginning. At the sign up they will ask your gender and what type of gender you are looking for. Then they will ask your postal code, followed by an email, password and finally your birthday. So honestly here you can lie about everything. Fake email and a fake birthday. But for our sake we will be honest except maybe on the birthday because we may be looking for younger so we will exaggerate that.

Next, we have ten random questions that we will have to answer in order to continue.

1. What is your body type? 1. Slim. 2. Athletic. 3. Average. 4. Stout. Let's say Average.

2. Do you have children? 1. No, 2. Yes, at home with me, 3. Yes, but they don't live with me. Let's say No.

3. What is your highest level of education? 1. No degree. 2. High school graduate. 3. Attended college. 4. College graduate. 5. Advanced degree. Let's say College Graduate.

4. What is your Ethnicity? 1. Asian. 2. Black/African. 3. Indian. 4. Latino/Hispanic. 5. Middle Eastern. 6. Mixed/Other. 7. White/Caucasian. Let's say Mixed/Other.

5. What is your Height? Let's say 5'10".

6. What is your Religion? 1. Agnostic. 2. Atheist 3. Buddhist. 4. Christian. 5. Christian- Catholic. 6. Hindu. 7. Jewish. 8. Muslim. 9. Other. 10. Spiritual. Let's say Christian-Catholic.

7. Do you smoke? 1. No. 2. Yes Socially. 3. Yes Regularly. Let's say yes Socially.

8. Next upload a photo to your profile. This is how people will see you on Zoosk.

9. Next you must verify your email.

10. Once verified you are in and it will tell you to follow the blue boxes to find and message singles using the box "Search".

Now we can start. Looking at the left side of the page you will see a "Magnifying Glass" with the word "Search" which allows you to look for specific people on Zoosk by profile name. Below that the "Carousel Button" that allows you to look at a variety of matches in your area. Below that the "Online Button" which tells you which profiles are actively online. Below that you will see the messages which is your "Inbox". Below that the "Connections Box" which shows you if any connections have been made to your profile. Below that the "Views Button" lets you know how many views you have had and finally below that the "Smart Pick Button" which is The Zoosk employees' recommendations for you. But first you must answer four questions that you can always change the answer to. Would you date some one that has children? Would you date a smoker? This one you can say I prefer nonsmoker but not against social smoker. Would you restrict your dating to certain ethnicities? Here you can pick from a list of ethnicities. Would you restrict your dating to certain religions? Here you can pick from a list of religions. But after filling these questions out the Zoosk team members will have a better idea of who to pair you up with. It's like an actor that has an agent. This is someone looking out for your dating career. There is somebody that gets paid to help pair you up and this site wants you to succeed.

Moving towards the right on the top you will see a "Heart With An Arrow" going through it. First, they will ask if you want a "Super Send" which means you can send a message to all the singles in your area and age range. At first it is free so take advantage of it. The questions range from, Do you have pets?, How old are you?, Or even hit me up if you want to strike up a conversation. There is a diverse list but only one choice, so choose wisely. Remember this is free and you can always change your message. They will ask if you want to boost your profile. Now this is an attempt to make money. You don't have to, but if you spare no expense then pay for the boost which means your profile will be seen by three times as much. 180 coins = $19.95. 480 coins= $39.95 which you save 25%. 1800 coins =$99.95 where you save 50%. All transactions can be completed by credit card or PayPal.

Moving on to the right of that heart with an arrow you will see a "Bell" that is your "Notifications Tab" which tells you who has recently viewed you. From there you can view who has viewed you and go on their profile. Below that there is an option that offers you to go "Invisible". This means you can view people's profiles and they won't know.

Now the upper right part of the page is the most important and needs to be set up immediately. It will show your "Profile Picture", a Zoosk member, your age and city you are in. When you see the "Arrow Pointing Down" click under the first option labeled "Profile". When you click this, it will take you to your profile page that shows a bigger version of your profile picture. Next to your picture it will ask you to name yourself. For example, I gave myself the name JackofHearts all one word which takes twenty-four hours to get approved. Under that it had my age and below city I was looking to date in. Then below that it gives you more options to add more photos. Below that is the "Verification Section" where you can verify your photos, for example take selfies so people know that is what you look like currently. Also, they will ask you to verify your phone number and Facebook and Twitter status. If you give your phone number that means you will receive texts from Zoosk. You may be overcharged if you overuse this service. Zoosk will send you an average of ten texts per month. But if you are an avid user your phone bill may be more than you expected. Zoosk will never Tweet or post to Facebook on your behalf.

Below this is your standard questions they asked you earlier such as gender, do you smoke with three more questions to answer. The first is relationship history such as divorce, widowed, separated never married, I'll tell you later. Now this can be an instant deal breaker for some people if they answer this. For me I put down never married, because I want people to know I have never been married. For a close friend I knew growing up he lost his significant other and he joined Zoosk looking for love. He put down widowed and immediately found someone that he has proudly been together with for two years. The second question they ask is what industry are you in or basically what do you do for a living? I believe this is important to put down, because I want to know what this person does with their time. Using me as an example I can put down hospitality which can also mean waiter and that could mean my nights are shot. Or I can put down Entertainment/Media which means actor and that can mean money if I am making it as an actor. A good friend of mine is a Nurse and put down Healthcare which can mean long and random hours at work. Is this fair for a possible significant other? Because you are looking to share your time and life with this person. The third question is the most personal. Income. It asks how much you make and gives you options in increments of from less than $25,000 to over $150,000. I have asked several people who used this site and they all say leave it blank. It is none of their business. Now some people may be turned off by this, because they have a specific lifestyle and can't deal with people living paycheck to paycheck. But most people believe a foundation must be built before personal questions are asked and answered.

Now to the right of these questions they will ask for your story and that is your bio which we have dedicated chapter seven to. Plug that in immediately. Below that they with ask for your perfect match. The perfect match is what you are looking for in a dater. This was mine for Zoosk.

"Looking for someone who likes to do anything LA. I want a partner who I can share my life with that I am crazy about and can become my best friend. We do our own thing and support each other for doing it and at the end of the day come together and enjoy life. I want to get married. I want kids. I want to start a family."

Now was this my mission statement. Yeah it was. I wasn't wasting anytime and this what I wanted. This was the bait I put out and I was going to see who was going to bite. Will it work? It has. It has gotten me dates and out of the house. Finally, they ask for the ideal date which is basically asking the question how would you impress me? You got to be witty here and creative. This was my Zoosk answer.

"Meeting for dinner and having a meaningful conversation where I want to know more. The night never ends, and I want to see you in my life for the rest of my life."

Now did it work. Hell, yeah and it still does to this day. It shows confidence and is right to the point. I don't want a one-night stand. I want a meaningful connection. Zoosk is that kind of dating site as opposed to Tinder which is more for quick hookups. Finally, they will ask you for your interests. This is where you plug in your favorite movies, artists, sporting events and the like. This is extremely important, because a lot of daters want to see if they have any interests in common.

Now moving down, the arrow you will have another option to go "Invisible". Below that was "Coins", "Account Settings", a "Help Button" and the "Log Out Button". The account settings button allows you to subscribe to Zoosk. Now you can do Zoosk for free, but I highly recommend you sign up for 1 months at $29.95. When you subscribe it allows you to send and receive messages, chat with your connections, unlock and connect with people who viewed you and say yes to and start chatting with your smart picks. Plus, all options have unlimited winks and messages. From my experience and the several people who have used this site you will make a connection instantly. Zoosk asks you to make one payment and it would be a waste of money to pay for three months at $59.95 when you are already busy dating someone. They charge $74.95 for 6 months and $149.88 for one year. Zoosk offers a "Help Button" which allows you to ask for tips on how to improve your story, ideal dates and perfect match.

When you look at the rest of the site it is all just pictures of the possible dates with their info right there. You can click on the "Like Button" or "Smile Button" for each profile you see. Also, you can send them an instant message or text and if they are currently online at that moment. You can simply choose yes, no or maybe.

This site is mostly a texting site and is one of the most successful ones to date. If your needs are to have a long-lasting relationship, then Zoosk is one you may want to consider.

CHAPTER TEN

BUMBLE FUCK!

I met her at work. We both waited tables in the same restaurant. She was half my age and beautiful. A "Chicago Girl" met a "New Yorker" and instantly there was a connection. She had a "Boyfriend" who called me four times in the middle of the night. The Chicago Girl didn't have a passcode for her phone and her Boyfriend learned a lot, but the most important thing he learned that night was he was out and there I was.

We hung out every day and became "Best Friends". She told me she didn't want a "Boyfriend" and I was cool with that. No labels, but we frequently kissed each other and told each other we loved each other every day as time went on. We went everywhere together, we worked together, and we eventually lived with each other. We never fought until I noticed these "New Friends" suddenly appearing in her life and mine. She was new in town and wanted to meet friends, so she signed up for Bumble the dating app before we had met and continued to use the app while with me. This would lead to us having numerous fallouts and eventually not talking to each other.

For the record I am not a fan of Bumble and I will explain why based on my experience and others I know who have used this dating app. Most of the people that sign up for Bumble are people with issues looking for other people to either help them or escape from their issues. But as you will find out in this chapter once these people invade your life with these issues, they fuck everything up you have going on! It is like an airport where people come and go in your life and then just disappear. I call them "Five Minute Friends". Bumble is known for this. It's not their fault, but as Tinder has a reputation for many one-night stands, Bumble attracts people looking for friends fast.

Me and her worked great together. I mostly went out of my way for her. She didn't have a car, so I took her everywhere. We always went Dutch, but we hung out all the time. This started becoming a financial problem for me, because I couldn't keep up. So eventually things started going wrong when she met friend number one from Bumble, we will call "Night Girl".

Night Girl had a job where she worked nights, dressed up very fancy and came home with a lot of cash she would flaunt in front of my "Best Friend". She was a shot girl that worked in clubs. Eventually Night Girl got my Best Friend the same job and started going out with her, dressing like her, and bringing home the same cash. About two weeks into their relationship I get a call early in the morning from my Best Friend. Now remember we are not living together yet. She is sobbing hysterical. In a nutshell she tells me Night Girl stole her purse when she was busy at work. She loses $800 and her ID. Night Girl is gone. Departed at 4AM to parts unknown. Her biggest concern is she doesn't have ID for NY to go to bars to see Bumble Friend number two we will call "Girl Friend" who she met before me. So as a "Best Friend" does, I came up with an idea to get her passport in two days. Of course, I drive her everywhere which includes Kinkos to print out her ID, DMV and finally the government building. Somewhere in all this chaos she needs a place to live.

So, she moves in to my one-bedroom apartment with her dog, a collie and my two Yorkshire Terrier dogs and me living rent free. One big happy family. She goes to NY to see Girl Friend with her new passport, leaves all her stuff in my apartment and leaves her dog with Bumble Friend Number Three "Second Choice Girl", which I will define in a minute. Of course, all I see is all her stuff all over my apartment, her dog is being taken care of by someone else and she is in another state with Girl Friend. While she is in New York she doesn't call me once and all her posts on Instagram were very close and sexy with her Girl Friend. Now we weren't a couple, but we were something and now living together, so yeah, my mind started racing. Was she using me? It didn't make me feel comfortable and it did bug the shit out of me. When she got home from New York she said she was using those shots on Instagram for her modeling career. She kissed me and told me she loved me, and I let it go. I was happy she was living with me and since Girl Friend didn't live in Los Angeles, I let that go. Honestly, I was happy seeing her every morning and we had fun living together.

So, my Best Friend starts her modeling career by setting up a photo shoot with Bumble Friend number four "Photo Girl". Photo Girl owned a camera, had a "Boyfriend That Was Homeless" and lived in a tent. Photo Girl either crashed on our couch, stayed with her boyfriend in his tent or stayed at home with her parents who didn't allow the Homeless Boyfriend over. Yes, these people were all in my life now. For a couple of days now and then my Best Friend would disappear with Photo Girl to go on these exotic photo shoots while I watched her dog and her stuff. Eventually there was a falling out over the price of a photo shoot and Photo Girl disappeared. I had to confront my Best Friend on her behavior toward me. She never wanted to discuss things and she never wanted to as she put it "create drama". My response was to let her know how I felt and make her aware of it.

So, my Best Friend continued working with her night job and would come home very late at night. She also worked at the same restaurant as me. She was a hustler. Her plan was to make as much money as possible and move back to Chicago in a couple of years to start a family. I asked her if I was in that plan and she said yes. Starting a family was never in the big picture for me. But recently my brother had started a life in Chicago by getting married and having a little girl. Plus, my folks had retired there so I was starting to get a taste for it. She was perfect. I am an actor in Hollywood and recently I had been doing well booking a national commercial that could make this move more financially possible. So, our plan was to be in Hollywood for two years, make bank and move to Chicago to start a family. This was the plan until Second Choice Girl, I had mentioned earlier, changed everything in one weekend.

Second Choice Girl had a "Boyfriend" who consistently cheated on her. A girl with very low self-esteem who sometimes went to my Best Friend's night job to work and never made money. Second Choice Girl and my Best Friend went everywhere together and were also "Best Friends". There were times where my Best Friend would take her dog and leave for days. The one weekend that changed my life was the one where I shot my national commercial on a Friday. That Saturday we both worked at the restaurant, she kissed me, told me she loved me and went off to her night job. Sunday morning, she comes home fucked up and she was supposed to work at the restaurant that morning. I do her a favor and work for her. Later that Sunday night we were going to have a celebratory dinner for my commercial. Just us! While at work I get a call from my Best Friend saying Second Choice Girl was finally dumped by her Boyfriend so my Best Friend takes her dog and leaves for three days. I get home and the place is just a mess. Her dog pisses everywhere and doesn't clean it up. I try calling her and six hours later she gets back to me saying she is at dinner with her "Best Friend". I look at her Instagram story and she's out with Second Choice Girl doing a "Boomerang Toast". I'm pissed! Was this just a story? Was she using me? My place is a mess! I left her a message sharing everything I felt!

She calls me the next day saying she is staying for a couple more days and doesn't like the way I talk to her. That I always have to know what is going on with her. That I am just her "damned roommate"! That was it. She was a different person now! Or was she always the same? I knew then and there she didn't care the way I cared about her. That's fine. But the money I was spending to keep up a relationship with her and the fact that she was using me and my place as a storage unit wasn't working for me. I called her and told her to just come get her stuff. She had the nerve to tell me I'll get it when I am ready. I took everything she owned threw it in trash bags and took a picture of it by my front door. She immediately got her stuff; numbers were blocked, and she moved back to Chicago. No more need for specifics. But how did this happen? The weekend that was supposed to be one of the best of my life, where I shoot the acting job of my life just ends with the girl, that I really cared about, gone from my life. Then I realized she was from Bumble and I just didn't see it.

Months go by and while I am visiting my family in Chicago we somehow get back in touch after a series of emails and Instagram phone calls. Part of me wanted to know what the fuck happened that weekend. I still cared about her and I wanted to talk. We see each other in Chicago the day after Christmas. I know everyone was saying what are you doing? I had to know some things, because I at one point considered a future with her. So, we make plans and she was supposed to pick me up and meet my folks. She was late in picking me up and I check out her Instagram story showing her picking up Bumble Friend number five "Last Minute Friend". Instead of picking me up she made other plans. She sees that I am checking out her story and calls telling me to meet her in a bar in downtown Chicago. So, I take an Uber and arrive forty minutes later. I find out Last Minute Friend was somebody she met on Bumble five days ago and they were meeting for a drink. So, this was the person you wanted to meet before me? The rest of the night she looked as if she was putting on a show of how great her life was by inviting "More Friends" to the bar and treating me like I wasn't important. At one point my commercial came on at the bar in front of her "New Friends" and it wasn't about her for a moment in time as they toasted to me. As the night went on all her New Friends disappeared, she gets tattoos done in front of me and she acts like I'm not really that important to her and I see it. I asked her if Second Choice Girl was in her life anymore and she said no. I ended the night by leaving. We had a few more falling outs with each experience ending badly and then eventually we stopped talking to each other.

So, let's sum up my Bumble experience. My "Best Friend" who I spent four months almost every day with, money with, worked with, lived with, fell in love with and considered a future with wants nothing to do with me. She introduced me to "Night Girl" who stole $800 from her and her ID. I race all over town to get her a passport so she can see her "Girlfriend" in NY while she uses my place as a storage unit rent free. Her "Photo Girl" is living with a "Homeless Boyfriend "and takes my "Best Friend" away from me for days at an end. "Second Choice Girl" gets dumped by her "Boyfriend" and it fucks up my weekend and my relationship. Yeah, all that shit happened with the cherry on top being her making last minute plans with "Last Minute Friend". But the foundation for this "Bumble Fuck Cake" was my "Best Friend" was the biggest "Bumble User" of all and created this monstrosity which fucked me over in the end.

Would I ever use Bumble?! Fuck no! It is the airport dating app. Where people come in from all walks of life, traveling to different destinations and then going to the next. People don't stay long in your life and they move on. But let us look at it further. I asked ten separate friends that used this app in their life and with their feedback I got an honest look. But before we start, one common behavior and fact about Bumble for gay guys and gay girls is you can message someone without matching. For heterosexual couples only the woman can make the first move by sending a message. If she doesn't send a message within a twenty-four-hour period after matching the connection disappears. And since the women has more control in Bumble, Ghosting is a common practice that occurs when all communication is ended suddenly in a personal relationship without explanation. Of the ten separate friends that I asked eight of them fell victim to this. Three of the most common tech problems Bumble has is one logging issues where there are times where the app will say cannot load or it will say there is a problem. Two the server connection is always going in and out like a phone with bad cell phone reception. Three is sending and receiving messages. Most of the times messages are not delivered and that creates a negative feeling for the dater trying to meet someone. But let's look.

So, when you start Bumble you have the choice of signing up with Facebook or your cell phone. I chose cell phone. Next, they tell you to enter a passcode. Once that is established, they will ask you what you want to be called, your birthdate and what your gender is. Now the gender even offers more options other than Men and Woman which includes Agender, Androgyne, Androgynes, Androgynous, Asexual, Bigender, Cis, Cisgender, Enby or FM2. Again, you can lie about anything here. Next Bumble will ask you to put up six pictures to get you started that you can download from Facebook or your own computer. Again, no verification so if you want to catfish someone very easy to do so. Next, they will ask you for your location so privacy is out the window here. But it will help you find people in your location. One good thing about Bumble is if you are across town it will adjust your location so you can date someone right by your location.

Once you establish this, they will ask you to be kind and sign a guidelines commitment. Now I recommend reading the guidelines before signing. But the gist of it tells you to behave on Bumble, no pornographic material, no kids by themselves, respect other people, and no pictures in underwear. They do state two things that doesn't guarantee it will be done which is posting your own photos and don't pretend you are someone you are not. They do have a verification for photos, but you don't have to use it. If you misbehave you are given a warning and then if it happens again you can be banned. They also mention that Bumble has three different types for users: "Bumble" for romantic interests, "Bumble Bizz" for business contacts and "Bumble BFF" is for making friends only. Now they tell you to respect each brand and not to cross over, but everyone does it in some form. Some people will start with BFF with the intention of crossing over for romantic. Or will start as Bumble Bizz but will roll into BFF. How do I know this? Of the ten people that used this app everyone was guilty of being a victim or even crossing over themselves. Remember you never know who you are talking to. But people do crossover, and this is a reason people flock to this site. It is extremely easy to get a quick hookup. Lastly, they tell you to send original messages to certain daters, but what most people do is copy and paste the same response to all the daters until someone bites.

Once you sign it you go to the next page which offers you either the dating option, friendship option or the business option. But before you choose in the upper left-hand side you can see your profile picture and edit your profile. First thing you will see as you scroll down is "Active Spotlight". This is how Bumble makes money and they use "Coins". They charge one coin to make you stand out in front of someone you like and two to make you meet great people in your area. They charge $34.95 for 30 coins and based on other people's experience save your money it is so not worth it. It is a waste of money. Second thing they will ask is if you want to "Manage Your Boost. Now the "Beeline" is the term they use to describe how many people have viewed you. If you pay $9.99 for one week you get this option and unlimited filters, rematches and extends. Now if you want to try Bumble, try the dating part. I recommend this for one week and go hardcore. Go out one night with the intention of going out to meet someone in an area that night or date people in that area that night. If that area doesn't work, you can try it again in another area. Otherwise Bumble will charge you $24.99 monthly every month until you cancel. Now I would recommend one month only if you are looking to make friends or even business contacts, but never the dating one. But on that note a lot of these accounts are not active, and Bumble is matching you up with nonactive accounts and it is there you are wasting your money. They even have an option for 3 months $49.99, $79.99 for 6 months and $119.99 for a Lifetime membership which is a waste of money, because after one week with this app people give up on it.

Next it is time to edit your profile. They will ask you to verify your profile, but you don't have to. Next, they will ask you to add up to three profile prompts. For example, they could be If I were famous it would be for...?? And my answer would be for holding my breath the longest underwater. Or two truths and a lie...?? And my answer is I am a published author. I am a fantastic cook and I know Tom Cruise. This is quick way to get people interested in you and show a side of your personality, but most daters feel it is not necessary. Next, they will ask about yourself which is your bio. Your education and job information. Then basic info that includes if you drink, smoke, political and religious beliefs.

Next mode is the "Settings Mode" and is the most important mode that you can change at any time. They will ask you what you are interested in men, women or everyone. Also, the age range you are looking for. Finally, the "Whole Country Mode" which you can break down by sliding the bar, but there is no mile indicator on it, so it is very vague. They also do offer a "Snooze Mode" so you can hide from daters at any time. Once your profile is set now, we can move into the dating portion called "Bumble Date".

Bumble Date immediately takes me to other people's profiles with the option of liking or passing and that is pretty much it. I can check out the profile, but the vibe I get, and most people get is they are using this for quick hookups. There really is no depth here. Yeah, I can read a profile and the person's interest, but I usually know just by the picture. "Bumble BFF" is for people that need to make friends. I set up my profile which was different from the dating one. But the vibe I got was desperation. Same went for the "Bumble Bizz," but it wasn't relevant for what we were looking for. But a thing to remember is if you swipe right and they swipe right then you have a match for twenty-four hours. Bumble is honestly only good for a week and then most people that have used it has told me they need a break from it.

At the end of the day Bumble has good intentions, but many flaws that doesn't have a great result rate. It is very easy to manipulate "the system" and it can mislead people looking for an honest relationship. There really is no depth and many people feel disappointed especially if they are paying $24.99 a month. Based on my experience and others it's a site for people that are new in town and lonely. "Five Minute Friends". It's a cluster fuck of people looking for a quick fix.

CHAPTER ELEVEN

GIVING THE DOG A BONE

Changing gears here. Many daters have pets and a belief that if you don't like their pet there is no chance in hell, I'm going to like you. But how about a website that allows daters and their pets to date other people and their pets. I am a dog lover and one of my deal breakers is if you don't like my dogs then I don't like you. But if you have a dog and I have a dog that get along and we want to find each other attractive where is this website? The following are the top five dating apps for dogs and their owners.

1. Dig-The dog premium dating app.

2. Tindog- Tinder for dogs and their owners.

3. Wowzer- Only for I-phone users but coming soon for android users.

4. Dog Date Afternoon-Only for I-phone users but allows adventure mode.

5. Meetup.com- A place where dog lovers can meet anywhere.

First let's look at Dig. The first thing you do is download the doggie dating app with either Facebook or Google. Then you set up your location and enter your birthday which can be whatever you want. Mine is always nine years younger, because I am looking for younger. There is no way anyone can verify this and hint everyone lies about their age when it comes to dating. Next, they will ask you a question if you are a man, woman or Non-Binary followed with a dog or without a dog option. So even if you don't have a pet, but love them anyway you can use this app. Next, they will ask you for a photo. My recommendation is going to your gallery in your phone and upload a picture with your pet and they allow you five others. My pictures showed me dressed up, running the marathon, me doing a reality show and me and my boys in front of the Hollywood sign. You can tell a lot about a person when they take a picture with their dog. Next, they will ask your dog's name and you can add up to six pictures and to classify if they are a small, medium, or large dog. If you have a second dog, you can add him later and up to six pictures as well with their size. Next, they ask you what you are looking man, woman, Non-Binary, or all with the option of with or without a dog, followed by the size of the dog you prefer from small, medium, and large.

Once you give that information the app is very simple. Starting from the bottom left hand side the word "Dig" appears. This is where you search for matches. Very similar to Tinder you will see a picture of the owner with the name and their location. Below that you will see their pet. Then there is a "Green Heart" that represents "Like", to the right a "Circle With A Slash" representing "Pass" and in the middle there is a "Star" which represents a "Special Like" that you can only use once a day for free so save it for the right one.

Now the only way you can make a connection is if a person you like chooses to like you back. Moving towards the center you see any possible matches that you may have. Moving to the bottom right is your profile picture. Once you click under that you can fill out a bio, your education, and your work information. Once someone clicks under your profile your bio pops up. That is pretty much it. You get ten choices they give you a day and then you got to click dig to look. Dig is one of the top doggie dating sites in the country.

From the dig app I was lucky enough to make two doggie dates happen. One was annoyingly scary and the second was an adventure with its own twist. The first story had me meet a single lady without a dog in the park. She was attractive, but she was really into my smaller dog Jake and not me or my other dog. I tried to make my moves, but she didn't seem interested. She eventually wanted to buy my dog Jake for five thousand dollars. Of course, I refused and left this lady sitting alone on a park bench. The second date was a real attractive woman that brought a French poodle. Our dogs start hitting it off. We start hitting it off. Two hours go by and I make the move by saying want to go to your place? She says it must be yours my husband will be home any minute. Now I had an opportunity, but I also a conscience. I left and she was extremely pissed off. After looking at her demeanor I could see I made the wise choice.

Second, we will look at Tindog which really is like Tinder for dogs and like Tinder most people are looking for a quick hookup with all parties involved. This was however difficult to download for Android. For I-phone it was doable, but I had to do some digging to find the actual Tindog app. Very similar to Tinder it requires a lot of swiping and it is very easy to get bored fast. The only difference this app asks is your dog's age and breed. It is addicting when it comes to swiping. But a big confusion with this app is people don't really know what this app is for. Is it more of an ice breaker for owners to use their pets? Honestly it just exists off its reputation for being an app for dogs. But most of the profiles I saw only had one picture and most of the bios weren't even filled out. It doesn't take much work to upload a picture and write a quick bio.

Wowzer loses half the population when the app is only available for I-phone users. Also, it is only exclusive to Seattle. But for the people that can use it do find difficulties with it. For starters it only allows you to add one dog. Secondly, very similar to Tinder when you swipe left it brings you back to your profile instead of going to the next dating profile. It does however allow you to create a profile for your dog that includes their name, age, breed, size, and a picture. It is more of an app for people that want to meet people that are dog lovers. Many of the users on this app don't even have a dog but use it to meet dog lovers. They consider the dog a "co-pilot" to meet someone else. My advice is this is not the app to use when meeting someone. You have a better chance going to the park and meeting someone with a dog. The app does allow you to make a profile and a tag line for yourself and your dog.

Dog Date Afternoon is very similar to the other dog apps that allows daters to see other single people with dogs. This app does allow the owner to have their own profile and their dog to have their own as well. Unfortunately, this app is only available for I-phone users. However, the best attribute for this app is it allows your matches to know when you are going on "An Adventure" like walk in the park or hike in the woods. Now "Adventure Mode" does give you a reason to go out and lure your match to your date. Honestly not the most attractive app, but it does stand out on its own and is worth a try.

Meetup.com is not a dating site, but a great idea to meet people with similar interests. For example, meetup.com has a group in Los Angeles that involves people that love Yorkshire Terriers. The people in this group have similar interests which is Yorkies and it allows your pets to meet other Yorkies. Plus, yourself a chance to meet someone yourself. You don't know if they are single or what their situation is, but you have something to talk about. By creating a community, you are creating a great energy for your pups and are allowing yourself the opportunity to improve your life. If they don't have your group, you can always create one.

Always use what you have to your advantage. If you have an adorable best friend this may be an honest way to break the ice and meet someone. It is a conversation piece and a reason to meet someone. Plus, you may be doing your best friend a favor as well. But remember after reading my stories there are some characters out there. Also make sure you when you take pictures with your dog that you cover their license up, because it may have your phone number or information on it. The last thing you want is a picture on a website with your information. You must think this way, because there are people that troll out there and look for your information.

CHAPTER TWELVE

HINGE ON

Hinge is the hottest and latest dating app when it comes to looking for a meaningful relationship. This is not the hookup app. The reviews are outstanding and people in their twenties and thirties are using it the most. What makes this app stand out more than the others is it puts everyone on the same page, and it is like Instagram profiles for dating that generates more conversations than any app. Instead of swiping you interact with the dater's profile directly. You can like any part of their bio or even comment on it to keep the conversation going. You must be on social media for this app to work. Hinge uses your Facebook information so you can match up with people who have mutual friends and avoids an ex or family related people. A couple of shortcomings Hinge does have is even though you can get a free trial they will hit you up with the $7.00 monthly membership fee, which honestly is worth paying. There really is no messing around on this app as people are taking it seriously and putting more into their profiles. Unfortunately, people who use this app may see the same people that they see on Bumble and Tinder. Pictures on this app are extremely important and really make this app work so they must be your best and most original. What some people use for this app is photofeeler.com where they have their pictures tested by others and you get honest feedback. You see what works for you and what doesn't. Another great quality about Hinge is they use video as well. Now let's open the app.

When you open Hinge, they will ask you to use Facebook or your phone number. To change things up I will sign up with my phone number. I can always link my Facebook account later for matching up. Once your phone number is verified, they will ask you to create an account or prefill with Facebook. I will create an account and they say Welcome to Hinge. The app design to be deleted. Right away they ask for your first name and an option for your last name. Last name is only showed to matches and is recommended for a more authentic and accountable community. Ok I am going in as Jack Benza which is my stage name for the last twenty years and a good way for someone to google me. So already this is a step up from any dating app we have used yet. Next, they ask you for your birthdate and they mention you can't change it later. Well I will stick with my traditional nine years younger so I can look for younger women. They will ask you to confirm your age. Next step is my email and I usually give my secondary email here. Next thing I see is a message that says adding basic info leads to better matches. Next it will ask you where you live, and you must give Hinge access to your location. Next is pick your gender which offers man, woman and the more option which offers more than sixty options which include the other or neither option. Next question is who I want to date men, women or everyone. How tall am I? What's my ethnicity? This also includes another option and I prefer not to say option. I chose the other option, because I don't want to label myself as White or Hispanic and Italian is not an option. What about children? The top portion offers the choices of don't have kids, have kids and prefer not to say. The bottom portion offers don't want kids, want kids, open to kids and prefer not to say. Where's my hometown? Where's my workplace? I'm going to say Actor/Bartender here, so she gets the lifestyle I live. Then they ask me what my job title is, and I put working actor. If she IMDB's me I have some credits. What I honestly like about this app as I am filling it out is there is a sense of truth here and I like the questions they are asking me. Next is where did I go to school? Next are my religious and political beliefs. Do I drink yes, no, sometimes or I prefer not to say? Same for smoking, weed and drugs.

Next, it's time to upload my best photos and videos by connecting with Instagram and Facebook. Hinge also requires that you add a prompt to your picture or video, so you stand out. Then they ask you to complete three more separate ones and give an answer for all three. Once I completed this I was immediately thrown into other people's profiles. Immediately a direction comes up saying if I like someone, pick something on their profile to like. Now be careful, because once you like something and send it the person's profile goes away, so make sure you look at their whole profile first before sending. One thing I noticed right on this website was the women were very attractive, so I wanted to do this right. So, I made sure my profile was top notch before I started browsing profiles.

When you look at the bottom left side of the page you will see an "H" and that is where you will able to see possible matches. Above the H there is an "X" and only push that if you want to move on to the next profile. To the right of this is a "Heart" where you can boost your profile for two hours and this is how Hinge makes money. One boost is $6.99. Five boosts is $5.99 each. 10 boosts is $4.99 each. Or you can upgrade and get twice as many dates with one month at $19.99, 3 months at $39.99 and 6 months at $59.99. To the right of this is the "Match Square" where you could click on and connect with your matches. To the far right is a "Small Figure" and this is where you set up your preferences. Right away you can set up your age range and underneath this you can set a "Switch" which signifies that you are serious about that.

Also, you set up your maximin distance with a "Switch" as well. You can also set up your religious and ethnic preferences. "Preferred Preferences" are offered but will cost you in order to let Hinge know your preferences when it comes to height, children, family plans, education, politics, drinking, smoking, marijuana, and drugs.

After that it pretty much is an upscale very simple app to use. The three things that make it unique is the prompts which are quirky one liners and the answers that you leave that make you stand out. The second thing is the videos bring your profile to life. Pictures are always nice to look at, but videos show behavior and is a step up from most dating profiles. The third thing is the fact that you can comment on any part of their profile. The only downside is you can only send one comment.

In the end I would recommend using Hinge for a month. I had two amazing dates on it where they both went to second dates. Both women were amazing and great looking. Unfortunately, one of the women didn't want kids and I wanted them. The other one just lived so far away, and it was very hard to see her with her job. But I got great feedback from it and I would use the app again. I realized that when I used videos it was just more impactful, and I got more responses. Some of my friends have used it and one is in a one-year relationship while the other just moved in with her match. It wasn't hard to get going when I started this app. It took ten minutes and now I am set up whenever I want to get serious and use the app. A term that Hinge did make famous in the online dating world is called "Kittenfishing" which is portraying yourself unrealistically in a dating app but in a positive way. Now this may be true for this app, but I honestly applaud the effort a lot of these people put in to make it happen. They care and so do I.

CHAPTER THIRTEEN

GO FISH

Plenty of Fish is a Canadian based online dating service that is free. It does make its money through advertising and premium memberships, but I want to again stress the word free. You get what you pay for. Now the reputation I get from this website is one of a bunch of characters looking to hook up. People that don't want to do much work, but don't want to miss the dating boat either. Before we even start, I must share with you three stories that happened to friends of mine while using this service.

1. While on a date an older female friend of mine met up with a gentleman at an upscale bar. This man ordered Johnny Walker Blue neat and drank it with a straw. The waitress even asked him if he was sure. For the record this shot will run you about $40.00 with tip.

2. While on a first date with my guy friend this woman pulls out tongs and uses them at the movies while they were both sharing a bucket of popcorn. My friend's hand was consistently in the bucket the whole time.

3. Towards the end of date after dinner a female friend of mine was getting dropped off home by her date. While driving home he turned on his Uber app and picked up a person while she was still in the car. The person they picked up was another female which he dropped off first before he dropped off his date. My friend was pissed off.

Now are these stories true? Yes, they are, and I have others, but the most important thing you must get from hearing these stories is most of these people really don't care. They just use the app because it's easy, convenient and people really have nothing to lose. It is the world's largest dating site so there is a great chance you will meet someone. Just who you meet may be not be the person you want. I call this website the "It is what it is" site. But it is ranked one of the top ten dating sites in the world with seventy thousand new singles joining every day on average.

When you first start the site, they ask you to make a member name, passcode, email, confirm email, gender, birthdate, country, ethnicity, verify some letters so you are not a robot and finally you have to sign an extensive agree to terms service. My advice is read this thoroughly before you sign, especially if you are female. There is this one part that reads Plenty of Fish does not provide background checks or identity checks. Why would they have this? Did some further digging, and I found out that Plenty of Fish is revealed as the most dangerous dating app in Britain as an investigation that links hundreds of rape, stalking, violent assault, blackmail, and child grooming. Plenty of Fish does provide safety tips in their extensive agreement which includes stay in public, provide your own transportation, know your limits, leave whenever you want and let family members know of your plans. It says everything except have fun. So, once you sign it then the fun begins.

First you must answer twelve quick questions to the left which are zip, city, gender, and height. What you are looking for which includes long term, hookup, friends, or dating. Followed by hair, body type, own a car, education eye color and second language. Next you must answer twelve quick questions to the right which include state, do you want children and have children, marital status, do you smoke, drugs, drink, religion, profession, and pets. Describe your personality in one word with most of the choices not matching you I just picked TV/film Junkie. How ambitious are you with several levels being mentioned?

After that you move down and answer more personal questions like when it comes to dating what is your intent with choices that include I want to date but nothing serious, I want a relationship, I am putting serious effort in to find somebody, and I am serious and I want to find someone to marry. Next is longest relationship I have been in and they ask my first name. Next, they ask for income that they only use for matching purposes. Remember that all fields are mandatory. Next, they ask about your parents if they are married or divorced and if you have any siblings. Followed by would you date anyone with kids, smokes and then they ask if you would date a "BBW", also known as a big beautiful woman.

Lastly, they will ask you to create a headline for example "Looking for me?" Followed by a hundred-word bio that will be the first impression when seeing your info. You can follow it up with your interests and then as an option you can fill out some conversation starters. Once you are done, they will ask you to verify that you are not a robot so you must give your cell phone number. Finally, they will ask you to put up an image of yourself. Here you can connect with Facebook and use an image from there.

Once the image is in place then I am sent to the main page. Right away I am staring at a seventy-three-question personality test which has the answer options of disagree, somewhat disagree, somewhat agree, agree. Now the questions they ask on this test are relatively boring and redundant, but this a tool they use to pair you up for matches. Some of the questions ask are I get nervous easily, I want my children to speak English, I have strong political beliefs, and my favorite Is my relationship pattern described as serial monogamy where I jump from one relationship to the next without a breather. Now some of these questions are out there and they may piss you off. But honestly it only takes five minutes and then you can get to viewing profiles. My recommendation is just getting it over with so they can start pairing you up and getting you going. But before you can they give you the test results, they have another test lined up for you. Why they give you test results for a test you really didn't want to take is beyond me. But in a nutshell the results told me.

1. Self-confidence: You feel very confident in social gatherings and I can interact well with others. Unlike some people I take responsibility for my actions.

2. Family Orientation: I value the company of family and domestic life. I take pride in keeping a good house, but while I am busy keeping a tidy home it prevents me from getting other jobs done.

3. Self-Control: As someone who exerts a fair amount of control over your actions you have the potential to stress yourself out too often. For example, you may be inclined to take more responsibility on projects, which always isn't necessary. Honestly this was balls on accurate. This really is me. I started taking this test a little more seriously. Maybe these people knew something I didn't and maybe they could help me meet someone.

4. Openness: I can look at problems any way and find a way to solve them. But I may be bored with projects that don't have intellectual stimulation.

5. Easygoingness: I appear to work very hard and accomplish a great deal. But the high standards I have for myself can frustrate my partner. This is true. I usually put my acting career first and I have heard this many times from past partners. I began to look at this test as extremely interesting, because no one ever really gives themselves a chance to look at things like this.

6. How does your personality affect your love life: The high standards I have for myself could frustrate my partner. I don't get along with everybody. I would be better off with someone who also has high self-control, so I don't get bored with my partner. My openness makes it easier for me to appreciate people that are different from me, but my openness might make it difficult for me to tolerate people that cannot appreciate diversity like I do. Yeah that was an eye opener and it made me rethink some things. I immediately took the next test. I was intrigued.

The next test was called The Relationship Needs Assessment that determines in detail a person's overt and hidden needs in a relationship. Also, this assessment provides users with highly specific guidance for putting results in practice. The user receives customized action plans that outline specific questions and topics for the user to ask or explore with potential partners. Best part this is all free. I started to really like this dating site. It had things to offer and I didn't pay anything. So, I took the test. And I realized the action plans are based entirely on the answer patterns I gave. There really is nothing like this assessment on the internet.

While taking the test they say there is no right or wrong answer. Be honest, take my time and if I am not in a relationship think about my past partner and use that. One hundred questions. The answers that can be given range from not at all like me, somewhat unlike me, somewhat like me and much like me. Questions ranged from: When I feel close to someone that person becomes an important part of who I am? It upsets me when I don't know all my partner's coworkers? I feel that conflict is a negative experience? And my favorite I feel loved when my partner celebrates my birthday with a gift? Ok after taking the test they broke it down into nine key factors with some example questions to ask myself.

1. Interdependence: I am highly interdependent on romantic relationships to a point where I even demand it. Keep your dependency in check so you don't lose your individual identities. Question I must ask myself: What degree of possessiveness do you think is healthy in a relationship? Honestly that was balls on accurate.

2. Intimacy: I need someone who will accept a slow pace for emotional intimacy with occasional reassurances about our relationship. Question I must ask myself: How often do you share the experience of meeting someone for the first time and trusting them completely? This does provide a freedom I haven't had in a long time.

3. Self-efficacy: I have tons of energy and confidence and I need a partner who feels the same way and not nurturing. Question I must ask myself: Are you the type of person who likes to get noticed in a crowd or not? I already knew this one.

4. Relationship readiness: I need somebody who is looking for a relationship rather than needs one to feel emotionally fulfilled. Question I must ask myself: Tell me what ways you are happy and successful single?

This was my last relationship in a nutshell, and this was a real eye opener.

5. Communication: I need someone who will eagerly give, collect, and discuss information patiently rather than giving it to me superficially. Question I must ask myself: Does the success of a committed relationship take priority over any aspect of your life? Deep stuff. Things to ponder.

6. Conflict Resolution: I need someone who will take time to find a complete resolution to a problem rather than finding a quick solution. Question to ask myself: Based on my experience does knowing to much about a problem help or hinder you from resolving it? Maybe knowing to much about something excludes your partner from the conversation.

7. Sexuality: I need someone who refers to sex as a meaningful sexual bond rather than spontaneous. Question to ask myself: Ask yourself if there is any difference between making love and having sex? Of course, there is. You want to make love to your wife.

8. Attitude towards love: You need to know the best kind of love grows out of a friendship. Question to ask yourself: Do you believe the best kind of love grows out of a friendship? My folks have been together for fifty-two years and they are best friends.

9. Preferred expressions of affection: Question you must ask yourself: Is it important to hear I love you every time you talk to your significant other? Yes, every time if you love them. Things happen in life when you least expect it. Life is short. It is a privilege to say it when you find it.

The third test they make you take is the thirty question Psychological test which determines what you really want as opposed to what you say you want. They ask at the beginning of this question: I want a partner who.... Some of the questions they use are: Holds a job that reflects success in their field. Has no credit card debt. Is interested in having sex frequently. And my favorite has no past relationship baggage. The answers they provide are Irrelevant, matters little, matters a bit, and must have. I took the test and here were my results.

First, they make you pick a gender. Then they break down this test for you by issues that lead to misunderstanding and conflict.

1. Accomplishment: a partner's economic stability. Level of success.

2. Physical Chemistry: what a partner looks like. The raw and physical attraction between two people.

3. Drive: a partner's mental and physical wellness.

What you say you want: Highly accomplished, strong valued, physical chemistry but not overly driven.

What you really want: An anchor which is well-poised to meet the hidden and unspoken needs you might be trying to fill in search for a relationship. The anchor represents someone who is willing to give you freedom and demands respect. Someone who is grounded and has a strong sense of identity and doesn't rely on you for economic security. Someone who is calm and low maintenance but is willing to try new spontaneous things.

The solution they offer is go fishing and look for words in profiles like family-oriented, sexy, experimental, capable, personable, and dependable. I get the idea for the test. It makes you rethink you making your own profile. Stepping up your bio with words people want to hear. Also, it changes your approach to dating. This is someone else looking out for your dating career. Another set of eyes.

Next is the twenty-eight question Keeper Test which measures if your love interest is a keeper. The questions they ask vary from: My love interest uses respectful language toward me. My love interest has a pet name for me. My love interest finds me extremely sexy. And my favorite my love interest loves holding hands with me. With the answers being provided being: Disagree completely, disagree, agree, and agree completely. Now this is more of a test of when you found somebody, or you can use your past relationship to see where they stood. The results showed an ABVE rating.

1. Aloof which in my case means she seems very independent minded and therefore may want independent autonomy from me in certain aspects of her life. Someone who can create and exciting love life, but it may be a challenge with this person.

2. Buoyant which means she is well centered and won't drive me crazy.

3. Virtuous means she tends to share your basic values on many life issues.

4. Expressive about her expressions and feelings. Easy to open to.

Result she was a keeper. Now I was getting tired of these tests, but I decided to give this site the full treatment it deserved so I took the final sex test. In this experiment it is a step by step guide on how someone would seduce you and you wouldn't be able to resist. Test results aren't shown on the profile, but it gives the taker an idea about seduction and helps the staff match you better. The gist of this test has someone flirting with you and you must pick three things that appeal to you and three that don't.

Examples include people which are witty, hard to get, appear sexy, or even mysterious. Then you add ways you would want to be contacted like phone, email, text or in person. Then thirty random questions will be asked where you agree or disagree. Some similar that you have been answering. Then you will be asked how a date should be structured spontaneous or planned? How long should a first date go? Choices are up to five hours. Then you will be asked how long would you take a first date? Choices range from holding hands, kissing, to intercourse or going with the flow. Finally, there will be several adjectives listed and you will be asked to pick from them with the possible answers being not at all like me, somewhat unlike me, somewhat like me, and much like me. Then it rolls into three topics you would talk about on a date and three you wouldn't. Three characteristics you like for your date and three you don't. Finally, they name places you would like to have sex, circumstances, and places you would like to have sex. With answers ranging from doesn't appeal to very appealing.

The result of this test is to find out how to approach me, how to date me, how to seduce me. It is extremely helpful and delves into detail. Rather than list my results I recommend jumping on this website and taking these tests for free you learn a lot. In a nutshell the results told me show tolerance and a sense of adventure. Allow myself to be allured recognizing that much of what they do is their need to be pleased. It gave great recommendations and strategies and I learned some things about my approach and what I wasn't doing right. Now that I completed all the tests it was time to look at the Plenty of Fish lay out.

When you first view the dating page you will see a lot of low scale pictures. I mean they are like last minute pictures where the person had ten seconds to put this picture up. Most of the pictures said "Online Now" under them so I could start connecting with them immediately which is a great thing for this site. Another great feature they have is an "Age Range Bar" above these pictures broken down from 18-24, 25-34, 45-54, 55-64, 65+ to view singles in your area. When I click under it takes me to their profile.

Each profile starts with the daters name and the tag line that I picked earlier which was Where have you been? On the left side is about: this says nonsmoker with Average body type. Below that is Details: 39-year-old, Male 5'10, Catholic. Below that Intent: Wants to find someone to marry. Below that Personality: Film/Tv Junkie. On the right side lists the city, ethnicity, education and profession. Below that are my pictures and then below that there is a feature where you can leave a quick message. So there really is no wasting time in meeting someone. Below that was all the questions I answered earlier when making my profile. One thing that did stand out was Needs Test and Chemistry sections had my test results and it allows other people to see my results. Yes, it is kind of personal, but this is how this site rolls. They really use these tests to help people get together. It does take some time to understand, but if you have time it is worth it. It is different from any site I have used. Below that is my bio and my interests I listed earlier.

Now when you go back to the main page on the upper left you will see an "Inbox" where you will receive all your messages. To the right of that you will see "Meet Me" which is where you upgrade your membership and you can see who wants to meet you. An upgrade will cost you $9.99 for an 8-month plan, $12.75 for a 4-month plan, and $19.35 for a 2-month plan. Waste of money don't bother. You can send a message for free. But the 2-month plan is not a bad idea to find out who likes you and give this site a chance. To the right of Meet Me is the "Search Button" which I believe is the best feature on this whole site you can break down who and what you are looking for specifically. That ranges from gender, age range, profiles with images or not, intent, body type, education, ethnicity, country, city, zip and miles you want them away. To be even more specific you can do an advanced search which is a complete profile breakdown to the specifics.

Above the search bar you will find a "Bell Icon" which gives you alerts if there is a match or if someone likes you. To the right of that is the token button that you can buy $16.90 for 10 tokens, $8.95 for 5 tokens and $1.99 for 1. To the right of that is the

"Profile Bar" where you can see what other people can see. Then to the right of that you can edit and add more pictures. Right of that the "Help Button". Right of that you can log out. In the middle of the page it says "Online" and that means you can start fishing and check out profiles. To the right of that is the "Chemistry Button" which means you can see the results from all your tests. To the right of that is the "Upgrade Button" where you will start paying for membership. This includes you show up first on "Meet Me". See if your emails were read and find out when someone viewed your profile. Waste of money.

Finally, the last section, which is above pictures, lists "My Matches" which is suggestions of possible matches Plenty of Fish provides. To the right is "Will Respond" which are more suggestions on people most likely to respond. To the right is "Sent Messages" and then to the right of that is my "Favorites".

This is a site that has volume and will keep anyone busy. The tests that I ended up taking are not mandatory but were extremely helpful. Remember this site is free and you can message anyone without spending money. I would recommend this site for two months, but remember you get what you pay for and there are some characters on this site.

CHAPTER FOURTEEN

REGULAR OR DECAF

Online dating has a reputation of being exhausting and very time consuming. Coffee Meets Bagel vows to change the way singles view online dating from it sucks to it doesn't suck. Their approach is to be different on purpose and make online dating more meaningful. Coffee Meets Bagel says Instagram and Facebook are blackholes that end in endless scrolling and staring of friends on vacations and cats playing the piano. When it comes to dating apps one in ten dating apps have people swiping over fourteen hours a week.

Coffee Meets Bagel takes the slow dating approach. Where quality is greater than quantity. Savor each meaningful connection and checking your potential matches should only take five minutes a day and then you are done. This site is strictly for long term relationships. "Bagels" are another name for potential matches and what Coffee meets Bagel does is offer you a limited number of bagels a day. Whatever you pick or don't pick this site begins to learn your type and the matches keep getting better every day.

Before we start there is some lingo you should know. "Suggested" are the most compatible bagels of the day that comes up every day around noon and it is one hundred percent free. "Discover" means you go in a section to see other matches that may not be compatible to you. You would need "Beans" in this section which is their word for money." CMB Premium" is the premiere section where you can see who likes you and if your messages have been read.

Coffee Meets Bagel has an outstanding reputation. First off ninety six percent percent of the users hold bachelor's degrees and of that one third of them holds a master's degree. It has a mutual friend vetting system that tries to link you with matches via Facebook. Messages can only be made if both parties like each other so there is a respect factor there. The best feature of Coffee Meets Bagel is they open a private line that allows you to talk to your match for up to a week without giving out your private line. If your bagel passes on you, they will never know that you passed.

Let's begin. When you first install the app, they will ask you Facebook or phone number, for this I will do Facebook. Immediately Coffee Meets Bagel will receive my name, profile pics, friends list, birthdays, and email address. They start off by saying all bagels will be available at noon daily and thus far they have made over eighty-four million matches. First, they ask me my name and then email. I used Jack Benza. They ask and say, just between us, marriage, a committed relationship, something casual, or not sure yet? I chose marriage. Why not? They respond, great you will fit right in! When would you like to settle down ideally? Choices were I'm ready right now, within two years, more than two years, not sure yet. I chose I'm ready now. Next, they ask me my gender. Next, I add my location by putting in country and zip code. Next, I upload a couple of shots with some captions added. Next questions were height, race, religion, job title, education, and what school.

Next, they take a minute so you can review your profile and fill out the prompts they give you which is very similar to the Hinge app. They say I am, I like, or I appreciate when my date, and then three ice breakers. Next, they ask what is my type and they talk about age range, height and how far do I want to look for matches that can range from ten to one hundred miles. Ethnicity, preferences, religion, and gender.

Next, they take me immediately to my first bagel which I can either not like or like and if I choose like, I can send an immediate message. The middle button is a "Skip The Line Button" which means I won't see that person for ten days. If you ever need to see your profile just check the upper left-hand corner, you can see your "Profile Picture". You can scroll to the right on your pictures and you can hold up to nine. Below that is your profession, school, prompts, religion, ethnicity, and employer. On the bottom right there is a "Pen Icon". When you click that you can go further and see your details and your suggested preferences.

On the bottom of the app there is the "Suggested Icon" which is where Coffee meets Bagel leaves their suggested bagels. To the right of that is the "Like You Icon" which shows matches that like you. To the right of that is the "Discover Icon" where you can explore profiles on your own, but it will cost you some beans. Bottom right is the "Chat Icon" and you can only access that when there is a match. The upper right-hand corner has a "Number" in the upper corner when you hit that it will ask you to buy beans. This may be an app where you have to spend some money, because the selections are very upscale and worth checking out. Beans go from 3000 for $24.99, 2000 for $23.99, 100 for $1.99. Now beans are used to strike up conversations with bagels under the "Discovery Icon". For example, one bagel I really wanted to talk to would cost me 385 beans to send a "Discover Like". Or you can even subscribe 6 months at $20 a month, 3 months for $25 a month or one month for $35. By subscribing you are getting to see who likes you, when your messages were read, and you receive 6000 beans a month. I would have to see how they match me up for a month before I throw any money down. In the meantime, I can always look under discover and see what is out there. When you first sign up, I was allowed two likes. After that I had to buy more beans.

But in a nutshell Coffee Meets Bagel is an upscale easy to use app, especially if you are looking for a long-lasting relationship. The options I saw were stunning. I believe the people that work for this app really want you to succeed. It honestly takes five minutes to go over their matches daily, which they have new ones daily and for an app that has over eighty-four million matches that is a great sign.

CHAPTER FIFTEEN

OK STUPID

OKcupid has many great attributes, but at the end of the day if you don't have a paid account you really can't do anything. So, for a dating site that calls itself free you're going to spend money. In 2004 the site was launched, and it took three years for it to become one of the best dating sites in the industry where thousands of applicants signed up. However, if you read a few reviews you will find them not so positive and a lot of the functions are not consistent. Let's break it down.

First thing you see on the homepage it is an interesting view of couples in humorous and romantic situations. You can see that the people at Okcupid care. Available on Android or iOS, the message sent is the dater gets noticed for who they are and not what they look like. Immediately they ask you for the ideal reason you are signing up for hookups, friends, short term relationships or long-term relationships. With a beautiful switch that asks if I am for non-monogamy. But before you sign up, they ask you if you are ok giving your location away, because they measure their audience. In order to continue you must.

Right away they ask email. Set up passcode and then they ask if you want to use the app or the site and I chose the app. Immediately they ask for your name, gender, birthday, and the question earlier what you prefer. I am looking for women. Of course, they give several other options. How old should they be? That is a great question, because that is how most people think. Remember people lie about their age, like I do so be honest what you are looking for and why. I am looking for someone that can give me a baby, so I am not looking for a woman in her forties. This is my Grocery List and that is on my Deal Breaker List.

Next, we start putting up to six pictures. Next give a short summary of yourself which is your bio you use on every site. Next it is time to answer a series of questions that will help calculate your best matches.

How long do I want my next relationship to last? Answers are one night, a few months to a year, several years, the rest of my life. I picked the rest of my life and then they ask how would my ideal person answer and I gave the same answer. Underneath there is a box that asks is this important to me and I checked it off.

Which word best describes you best? Carefree or Intense and I chose intense. I chose my ideal partner as saying intense.

How important is religion/God in your life? Extremely important, somewhat important, not very important, not important at all. My answer was somewhat important, and my ideal answer was not very important.

Are you ready to settle down and get married now? Absolutely, no way, get married yes, settle down no, get married no, settle down yes. My answer was absolutely, and my ideal person would say settle down yes, marriage no.

Do you enjoy discussing politics? Yes or No? Me no and her yes.

Would I date someone in considerable debt? Yes, it is not a problem for me, Yes, If I thought the debt was justified, or No. My answer yes not a problem. Ideal answer yes if it was justified.

Is astrological sign at all important to you? Yes or No? No to both.

Do you smoke? Yes, no or rarely? Rarely for both.

Which best describes your political beliefs? Liberal, Centrist, Conservative, Other? My answer other and ideal answer liberal.

Can you date someone who was messy? Yes or No? No to both.

Which would you rather be normal or weird? My answer is weird and ideal is normal.

Are you currently employed? Yes, full time, no, part time, I am a student. My answer full time. My ideal answer is full time and I marked this as very important to me.

Could you date someone who does drugs? Yes, yes, but only soft stuff like marijuana, No. My answer no. My ideal answer is Yes, but only the soft stuff.

Choose the better romantic activity kissing on Paris or kissing in the woods in a tent?

Both answers are the woods.

Is jealousy healthy in a relationship? No on both.

Lastly, they ask to verify your phone number so when you sign in you can use your number and now, I was in. Immediately they take you to main page where you see one profile and the ability to "Like" or "Pass". Each profile has a picture of a percentage of how much of a match they are for you and a bio. Upper left-hand side is the "Double Take Icon". One great free feature is "Double Taken" which sometimes doesn't always work, which means it acts as insurance. It uses what you filled out in "Looking For" section and it tries to send you newer people that they think might match up with your ideal match. It is a great way to find more profiles you would have found during browsing. It also gives more information and pictures than regular matches. On the desktop it is more visible, while on the phone app it is not. Above that is a "Magnifying Glass" where you can search for more profiles. If you want a more in depth search you can break it down by special blend, match%, distance or last online. To the right of that is the "Chat Icon" where you receive messages from daters and the Okcupid staff. When I went to this icon there was a message from the staff that gives some pointers for the app by saying to replenish pictures, answer all the questions so daters can know more about you and share interesting facts about yourself on your profile. To the right of this icon is the "A-List Feature" where you pay to see who likes you, intros, and matches. To see who likes you press that icon and you will see that they charge $9.99 a month, $13.33 for 6 months, $13.33 a month for 3 months and $19.99 for one month. "Intros" are daters attempts to spark a conversation with you. "Matches" are any possible matches you may have and when you pay you can send a message. When you first start, they give you the ability to send a message to any possible matches. The first person I liked then became my first match, so I sent my message to them. When I looked at her profile, they compared my answers to the questions I answered in the beginning and compared it to her. This is how they get the percentages with matches. Once I sent a message they said if it's meant to be you will hear back. Until then you won't be able to view their profile or see that message.

Finally, to the far right you can review your profile. I recommend checking it out, because there are still questions and things you must fill out to make it complete. You must add in height, body type, do you smoke, marijuana, drink, diet, do you have kids, want kids, and have pets. Also, there is the option to go "A-list" or get a boost.

A fun feature is they ask you questions like: What is your current goal, I could beat you at, My golden rule, I value, The last show I binged, A perfect day, The most private things I am willing to admit, What I am actually looking for?

They have a great ice breaker technique. All of these they give you options you can choose from. What is your ideal virtual date? This is broken down into several questions that ask: If I like phone sex, What is my favorite type of date, Is love important and What is your quarantine personality? This area is extremely extensive, but necessary if you want to find a match. There are like thirty extra questions in this section. Finally, you can show off pet or vacation pictures. But when I did this, I had difficulty getting on Instagram which they recommend, and I had to use Facebook.

    This app was extremely basic and every time I move to a new icon, they asked me if I want to continue with the app or the desk type site which was becoming annoying. Stupid when they consistently do it. Also, they tell you to browse even when your profile isn't fully complete. Also, the only way to send a message is pay and when you pay you can't see that person's profile again unless they answer your message. I almost ask the question is it even worth sending a message? It gives the impression that I am not worthy enough to send a message. I would give it a month and spend the money. The percentage thing works and is their best feature. If you pay for the A-list, then you can see who is viewing you and that is your best chance to meet someone. I have had several people join the A-list and use the percentages to meet people right away. That is the reason people use this app. You get nine free likes a day and then you must pay. The numbers are right there, and people take advantage of this. But honestly this is more of a hookup app when you look at it. People pay $9.99 a month just to send a message. It is a basic app, but it doesn't require a lot of work. Like Tinder it is extremely fast and to the point that anyone with half a brain can use it. It is an extremely liberal site that asks you questions about gun control and political questions that will never stop. I couldn't even get through all the profile questions. I felt the staff had enough info for matches and there was no indication of when it was going to end. It became stupid after a while.

CHAPTER SIXTEEN

SNOOTY BOOTY

Are you looking for that highly motivated and educated someone that ranges from thirty to fifty years old? But the only way you can meet this person is by taking a comprehensive personality test which happens to be the foundation for our latest dating site. Available as a desk top site and a dating app, EliteSingles.com focuses on serious relationships and a lasting connection. Globally over sixty-five thousand members join every week and eighty percent of the applicants have college degrees, which strive for a more intellectual individual. The site has a phenomenal reputation and matches peoples on personality.

Besides going for the intellectual connection EliteSingles.com matches on the financial aspect as well. What you do for a living counts. Besides answering standard questions, you will take a twenty-two-minute personality test that will measure twenty-nine different traits. If you are a standard member you can send

"Winks" and do extensive browsing, but if you want to make an impact, especially on a site that matches you financially, you must spend some bread. If a paid member sends you a message you can't answer them unless you are a paid member. Any members can experience the "Have You Met" section that allows you to view an entire profile and decide if you "Wink" or "X" them out. Finally, the Big 5 Personality Dimension Analysis breaks down each member's personality based upon Conscientiousness, Agreeableness, Openness, Extraversion and Neuroticism.

So, as we sign up, I give the traditional information of man looking for a woman, email and I sign the disclosure. I give my age and they ask how important is your date's age with answers ranging from I don't care to extremely important. Marital status. What I do for a living. How important is your date's job. Height and her height. Next, they ask random questions by showing pictures and say pick a spontaneous shot and what season inspires me. I didn't know if this is part of the personality test. Religion. Appearance. Of course, every question is followed by how do we feel about my date's beliefs or looks?

Moving on I was being asked questions like, do I feel overwhelmed with answers ranging from it doesn't apply at all to completely applicable. I realized I was in the personality test. It continued with I often try to make sure other people feel good. Now I will list random questions that I feel standout. For the record I would really do this site, because I am not a really the most financial and intellectual guy. But for the sake of this book and because I am curious, I will give this site one hundred percent effort and see if I can land a match or even a date. The test continued with I consider myself to be trendy. Wow this is a long test. What I did notice as I was taking this test was the "Status Bar" so I could see my progress.

So, as I progressed during the test, I noticed they asked a lot about certain words that I felt. Like secure, happy, or confident and this was a third of the test. Finding the right words. They do ask two to three things I am most thankful for. I mentioned family, friends and career is what I chose. Very personal questions that were very similar to other sites like habits. They ask for your name or nickname and location. Then they ask about your date's location and how important it is to you. Next, they ask about my financial income. I finished the personality test with ease and then posted some pictures. Right away I was pushed to the membership page. $34.85 a month for 3 months, $19.95 a month for 3 months and 17.95 a month for 12 months. Or you can press the "Continue Button" to move on. This was kind of pricy compared to other sites and it wouldn't let me leave the page. Memberships include unlimited communication, view all member photos, read all receipts for messages, and get an extra twenty wild card matches a day. Now this didn't seem worth it. I exited the page and signed in again to see if I could go check profiles and it worked.

Starting at the top from the left is your "Inbox" for messages. Next to it is your "Matches Icon". Once you click your preferences are listed on the left and to the right your matches but blurred out. The funny thing is you can send them icebreakers and smiles, but not a message unless you pay. To the right I have the "Visitor Icon" which makes you see who visited you, but you can only see who they are by becoming a member. To the right of that you have the "Have You Met Icon" which again only available for paying members. To the far right is the "Profile Icon." This is where you can add more pictures and go over your preferences.

Eventually I paid for a month with a friend of mine and I got several matches from nice women. I ended up going on two dates and they expected me to pay and I did. These were expensive dates and these women were high maintenance. However, my friend took a lady out and is currently in a relationship with a woman he thought was out of his league. Which shows that anything can happen if you just get them out on that date. This is an extremely easy app to use with high standards and you need to spend money to get things going.

CHAPTER SEVENTEEN

FATAL ATTRACTION

Life is short. Have an affair. The dating site Ashley Madison encourages people to sign up and get something on the side. 5.2 million people have signed up for this site. Most of which are single people looking for someone that is attached. It only takes thirty seconds to sign up and get going. Immediately they ask are you an attached male seeking females, attached females seeking males, single males seeking females, vice versa, males seeking males and females seeking females. Member name, no passcode, country, zip code, date of birth, ethnicity, and email.

It takes a total of five minutes to fully answer a few questions without filing out a profile. Anyone can sign up for free and check out all the local members. Immediately you get specially selected locals with their preferences listed and their location. Some have photos while others don't to remain anonymous. If you decide to not post a picture there will be a badge that says please respect my discretionary requirements. I decided not to post a picture. Right away there is constant chatting going on as you are looking at profiles. You can send "Winks" and get the chats going. Unless you are a member you cannot exchange emails or start chats. What a lot of people do is hang out on the site and wait for people to show up or start a chat.

Ashley Madison does offer features where you can share private photos with someone that shares their "Key" with you. But you don't have to share this feature as well. You can stroll right in without spending money and not giving any private information. Right away they are asking why I am here and what I am looking for. Choices are undecided, anything goes, whatever excites me, short term, long term and cyberaffair/erotic chat. I chose undecided. Then they ask height, weight and an opening line greeting where I said," Life is short especially these days.". My greeting was "I am new to the site. Just curious and looking around.".

When I entered the site, I saw many blurred pictures. People were covering their face but were showing specific body parts they were proud of. But there were some interesting profiles and I saw a life I am not used to. Some people had several pictures where they were doing yoga and putting themselves in positions that would get the imagination going. Each profile gets a "Request Access Key" which means if I click on then I get to see the private pictures of that file. If they click on mine and I have pictures same goes here. Most of these pictures were people wearing masks. Some of these pictures were blatant and didn't give a fuck what people thought. A lot of undecided people just hanging out waiting. It was kind of trippy. Also, every profile has a bio and the greeting. Some of these were sexy as hell such as sway me, I am so damn curious, give me a reason, and sweets wanted. This was a one-night stand world. The "Discovery Icon" allows you to peruse the site and I recommend checking it out just for fun.

It is pricey though basic service is $59.00 for 100 tokens, classic service 500 credits for $169.00 and elite is $289.00 for 1000 credits. What do you get? Well the three most important things are unlimited email messages to up to twenty members. You get to check all the hidden pictures members have. You get unlimited chats with all the clients. One more feature is everything remains anonymous. If after the three months the user still hasn't met someone in person to have an affair, the user can then apply to get their $289.00 refunded to them. The site accepts credits cards, PayPal, mail, courier, or Western Union as payment.

Ashley Madison makes it easy to connect with people if you purchase a membership. Privacy is a given and the more you share, like pictures and correct emails you can get something out of this website. People clearly lie on this one as you can see pictures of people and the age doesn't match up. But there are defined characters that don't mess around here, and they know what they want. In the disclosure you sign to log on they say they don't do background checks on this site. There is a filter under "Discover" that you can use to work on age range and specific location range to meet people. There is a high number of members. It is suggested to take some time and look around to see how many other paid users are on the site. Also, how many are active users that have logged in in the past month. Another review suggests that most of the female members are fake, so you should be hesitant before you spend that money.

Websites like this exist and there people out there that like to role play or simply can't stand the person they are with. The best thing about these websites is you can give all fake information and window shop for as long as you want and then just disappear. The funniest thing is recognizing someone from these sites and them confronting them in real life. It has happened and makes an interesting conversation. Another thing to remember is these people can be anyone with malicious intentions in mind. Now of course this can happen to any dating site. So be careful about sharing specific information. In 2015 Ashley Madison was hacked and all the private information of the members was stolen.

CHAPTER EIGHTEEN

GOT A MATCH?

Match.com is a user-friendly dating site that has been around for twenty-five years which centers on long lasting relationships without the pressure of marriage. Based on its reputation it consistently guarantees that you will find someone within six months and if you don't, they will give you six months for free. More than ninety one percent of the clients have bachelor's degrees. They have an estimated thirty-seven million viewers a month, so traffic is not a problem. Forty four percent of the clients are women with it being more dominated by men. The profile will take about ten minutes with the basic questions and habits we have been answering throughout this entire book with preferences. Match.com knows your romantic partner should also be your best friend. They allow you to specify what you want in a partner. If one of your deal breakers is not smoking, they won't even pair you up someone like that. You choose the same personality traits that you are looking for in a partner. They implore that someone who shares your values is just as important as finding someone with good communication skills.

Let's begin. Immediately Match.com has a home page with pictures and profiles. Top three questions. What are you looking for man, woman, man to man, woman to woman, age range and zip code? Right away down to business. Right away you are looking at profiles and it is free to look, but to sign up you must give your email, age and first name. This is recommended if we are going to move forward. Now the standard questions height, never married status, have kids, want kids, smoke, drink and education. Next, they give you a wide selection of your interests that you can pick from.

Moving forward they ask if you are looking for something specific and this is where you get your Grocery List out:

- ✓ Age: You set the age range.

- ✓ Height: You set the bar.

- ✓ Body type: Very specific where you can pick slender, athletic, about average, curvy, big and beautiful, a few extra pounds, heavyset and there is a "Must Have Button" for this. You can pick as many as you want.

- ✓ Should you date want kids: No, definitely, someday, no preference. This is a must.

- ✓ Should your date have kids: No preference. No kids. Yes, but not living at home. Yes, but at home sometimes, yes and should be living at home. This is a must.

- ✓ Ethnicity: with a must option. White, Native American, Other, Asian, Hispanic, Middle Eastern, Black/African, East Asian you can pick as many as you want.

- ✓ Drinking: No, socially, moderately, regularly.

- ✓ Education: No preference, high school, some college, Bachelors, Associates, Graduate, PHD. You can pick as many as you want.

- ✓ Religion: Agnostic, Christian, Buddhist, Hindu, Jewish, Muslim, Spiritual but not religious, Atheist, other. You can't pick as many as you want.

- ✓ Smoke: No preference, no, yes sometimes, yes daily, yes trying to quit.

- ✓ Marital status: Never married, separated, divorced, widowed.

Ice breaker time. Now they want you to pick a topic and make a first impression. There is a wide selection to pick from. They vary from: If I had three wishes, one thing I am working on improving, The one thing I would like to change about the world. I chose three wishes and said. First wish a date with you. Second wish you have an amazing time. Third wish is the second date you have the time of your life. After that you get to pick two more topics.

Next you put up a photo up to six that you can upload or use Facebook. If you become a full-time member this is what comes with the membership: chat with local singles, send and receive messages, see who has viewed you and attend in person events, which is something a lot of dating sites don't offer. Now there is a premium plan and a standard plan. The difference between the two is with premium there is more savings, monthly boosts one profile review a year and message read alerts.

- Premium Plans: Best Deal-12 months, $21.99 per month save 56%.

- Most popular- 6 months, $24.99 per month save 50%, 3 months, $39.99 a month save 20%.

- Standard Plans: 12 months, $20.99 a month save 53%.

- Most popular- 6 months, $22.99 a month save 49%, 3 months, $35.99 a month save 20%.

All subscribers also get a super like, send likes, see who has liked you and remove members from your view. Now at this point they will ask you to pick a membership but at this time you don't have to, and you can start viewing the site.

In the upper left-hand side, you will see the "Discover Button". When you click on this you will see your top picks of the day. Each top pick has a picture, the percentage of how compatible you are and a profile. But before you start looking at these take a look at what the site looks at, finish your profile and then you can give yourself an honest approach. Once you do go back and look at your choices. If you like someone you can send them a message.

To the right is the "Search Button" which consists of the basic search. A "Mutual Search" which is people you have things in common with based on what you said in their profile. A "Reverse Search" which shows people looking for someone like you based on what you told them in your profile. A "Saved Search" which is people you have looked up before.

To the right of that is the "Likes Button" which shows you how many likes you have. If you are a member you can boost your likes which means you will get four times more views when your profile gets pushed to the top for sixty minutes. The prices for boosts are 10 pack for $3.00 each, 5 pack for $4.00 each and 1 for $4.99 each. Pay pal or credit card. Also, under this button is the phonebook mode with is "Matchphone" where you can receive calls, texts, and emails as a member. When you subscribe you get all these offers and the charges are part of the premium or standard plans. To the right of that is your "Inbox" for any messages. To the right of that is "Live Events" for Match paid members that you can attend.

To the right of that is the "Profile Button". This is where you can finish your profile, bio and any questions that you still need to fill out. These include stance on marijuana, exercise habits, hometown, pets, political views, school, work details and languages I speak. Also, on this section you can see how many people has viewed you. There is also a "Safety Section" where you can report profiles that act inappropriately. To the right of that is your "Settings Button" where you can manage things like blocking people, change your subscription and receive help from Match.com.

Match.com is a website/app where the chances of meeting someone long term are great. It has the reputation and the guarantee of meeting someone. It was fun signing up and going through the profiles. No one on this site is wasting time. It feels safe and very professional. There is a lot going on. They do give you five free messages when you start. I recommend spending some money for at least three months. The boost does work, but you must be online for that hour to see some quick response. I like the fact that you can call people and that they verify your number. At the end of the day there are more chances to meet more people in bulk if you want a long-term relationship.

CHAPTER NINETEEN

LIVING IN PERFECT HARMONY

You want to get married? This is the website/app for you. A website that has the highest success rate for this. The many people that have used this website/app are married with kids, married in a long-term relationship or are just genuinely happy. eHarmony is a dating site that aims to help its users find the best match for them using a compatibility matching system which can narrow down each person's match to the fewest possible matches. Since 2000, eHarmony has been providing matching connections all over the world. The site was founded by Dr Neil Clark Warren, a clinical psychologist dedicated to find better ways to find love. The site creates around fifteen million matches a day, and more than six hundred thousand couples got married because of it.

eHarmony has a good reputation that uses sixty-six million members in over two hundred countries worldwide. The gender distribution consists of most of the members which are those who are twenty-five to thirty-four years old. Its members are quite active, looking for a serious relationship, and are in the age of settling down and starting a family. You need the premium upgrade so you can use it efficiently. People who stay on this site have most likely upgraded their account.

The registration process takes a lot longer compared to other dating sites. First the site gathers all the important information from their users before they can browse and look for matches. Let's get started.

When you first sign up for eHarmony, they give you the option of a man looking for a woman, vice versa or same sex options. This is mostly a heterosexual site. eHarmony did launch Compatible Partners in 2009 after a lawsuit which services the gay and lesbian community. But now when you log on, it does give you a same sex option. After that I leave my email, they immediately throw me into the Compatibility Quiz. This is what the quiz measures:

You're learning more about your matches, discover more about yourself too. The eHarmony Compatibility Matching System works with your personal quiz results to give you a Personality Profile. The profile is the basis for your matches and gives you the insight into your own preferences and personality. They say it takes about twenty minutes. Be spontaneous. There are no right or wrong answers.

After the quiz is done, they will show me any possible matches based on my answers. I am going to list random questions on this test with the possible answers, so you get an idea of what they ask.

Regardless of where you live now, where are you most likely going to live? In a large city. In a suburb. In a small quiet town. In a rural area. It doesn't matter where we live if I can do a lot of traveling.

In addition to love and affection what are the main reasons for wanting a relationship? You can pick up to three answers. Life is easier with a partner. Emotional security. Having a partner, I can trust. Frequent intimacy. I want someone to spend my free time with. So, I'm not alone. Security.

Let's say you and your partner are invited to a friend's wedding. As you are getting ready for the party, which thoughts are you most likely thinking? Are we going to look together? Have we brought the right gift? Will there be too many people I don't know? I notice that I really don't like dressing up.

Why do you think you are single? I have very high expectations of the person I will spend the rest of my life with. I wasn't ready before now. I am too shy to meet people. I haven't had the time to date. I just don't socialize much.

There are five steps to this test. After fifteen percent of the test they move into my preferences part of the test.

What do you think is most important in a relationship? You can pick up to two.

Giving each other a lot of space. Considering each other in what you want. Not examining everything in depth. Making life easier and peaceful for one another. Accepting our imperfections. Always trying new things. Sticking to a routine.

After showing me some images and shapes I was halfway done. Now they were going to ask me about my habits.

Are you easily excited about things? Not really. Yes often.

After the quiz is taken you will be asked to fill out the basic information, name religion, occupation, do you want kids? And income which ranges from $60,000 to $125,000, $125,000 to $250,000. Over $250,000. Some of the questions have a "Lock" next to the question and they only appear for eHarmony staff like last name, what you make and zip code. Next, they have me upload a photo. They will be clear for members and blurred for no members.

Next you must set up two questions about yourself that you must answer which consist of: I like to spend my free time. I have a passion for. The first thing people notice about me. Then you must set up a bio that consists of what you are looking for in an ideal mate. Now that I was in, I was able to see my matches and the main page. Immediately I went to the upper right-hand corner to check my profile and put in the right picture I wanted and add more pictures. Then I had to answer more questions under my profile. First, I had to come up with a personal quote and what I was thankful for. Best life skills and things I can't live without. My friends describe me as. Then I must scroll over to the right and fill out all the personal questions we have been doing in all these sites.

Below that I was able to see the results of my quiz. Not the easiest results to read but this is what I got. The fundamentals of my personality, intellect, feelings, and instinct are normal and say that I can deal with any given situation. To see the rest of my results I would have to become a member. Lastly, I set up my phone verification with eHarmony. Above this "Profile Icon" is another button that says, "Dating Tips". These are articles that eHarmony provides to help you through rough patches. There was one article that listed how to get over someone that is not good for me. Helped me out tremendously.

To the left of this is the "Subscribe Button" and what you will pay if you are a member.

- 6-month Premium Light Plan goes for $65.00 a month you get to view unlimited photos, unlimited messaging, see who's viewed you, distance search, detailed personality profile.

- 12-month Plan Premium Plus is usually $45.90 a month, but a special is run where it will only be $22.95 a month for the first three months when you sign up in the first 35 hours. Get same features.

- 24-month Plan Premium $35.90 a month but 50% off the first 3 months when you sign up first 35 hours for $17.95 a month with the same features.

To the left of the "Subscribe Button" you have a "Message Button". To the right of that you can see your "Matches Button".

This is where you can see your matches, but very important you must set your preferences otherwise you will get matches from all around the country. You must click under matches and then go to the right side that says, "Match Preferences". You must fix where you want to search, your age range, want children, do you want to date anyone that has children and smoke preferences. Premium services can put in income, religion, ethnicity and then education. Also, to the right of the match preferences is the "Sort Button" where you can specify your search by registration date, distance, compatibility score and last log in only available to members. Matches can also see who viewed your profile and profiles you visited.

Finally, in the upper left there is the "Home Button" that takes me to my profile. Underneath my picture there are five icons from left to right which are "Messages", "Matches", "New Visitors", "Profile Completion" and "Verification".

Now I was going to sign up for real. I looked at what was available and that 50% deal. The total was going to cost me with the discount $481.95 for one year broken down into three monthly payments. I did it. I signed up for a year. The final thing it told me to do was find love. I felt like I took a huge step today. I was now invested and all I had to do was meet one person and make a connection. Just found out I can have a beta video date as well. Now this was all going on during the Covid-19 period which I will cover in the final chapter. But I am really excited I signed up, especially for this one.

CHAPTER TWENTY

THE DAILY GRIND

It is the most popular dating app in the gay, bisexual and bi-curious world. Grindr is more known as a hookup app. Ever since 2009 over two million people daily use the app across one hundred ninety-six countries. Grindr is the mostly known as an all-male dating app all looking for one great night. The good thing about Grindr is it is local, free, and anonymous. The bad thing about it is the reputation is not known for long term relationships, but casual.

Signing up for Grindr is very fast and easy as the app asks for your general information like username, email, and age, which legally must be eighteen. Then it will ask specific preferences that refer to age, location and which "Tribe" do you belong to. A tribe refers to your selection of identity categories and sexual interests that you use to label your profile. I asked a couple of my friends who use Grindr and they say the categories overlap and step on each other. They are not accurate, and many profilers get confused and disappointed.

The tribes they mention are:

- Bear- A husky large man with a lot of hair.

- Clean-Cut –Is a military look.
- Daddy- Is a middle-aged man who has a dominant personality.

- Discreet- Means someone who wants to stay in the closet and does not want his info getting out.

- Geek- A gay man with enthusiastic knowledge of sports and activities or intellectual pursuits.

- Jock- Gay man with an athletic build.

- Leather-Gay man wearing only leather as a sexual fetish and performs acts.

- Otter- Thinner and hairier gay man.

- Poz- Is anyone HIV positive.

- Rugged- Rough hairier gay man.

- Trans- Is a transgender person.

- Twink-Younger and thinner gay man with no hair.

What gets confusing is gay men assume and expect that tribe. Men may assume seeing a skinny guy that he is a Twink and must be feminine, but he may identify as masculine. Or when you think of a Geek, I would imagine a cute smart guy and not the guy who loves sports. What image was Grindr going for? Also, there are all types of transgenders and what they do is throw them all under one category. This leads profilers to believe that a trans man or trans woman cannot fit under the category of Twink or Leather. Profilers can only pick one tribe, but if you become a Grindr extra and pay the $5.00 you can pick up to three tribes.

Next create a short bio in the "About Me Section" which will hook in your users. You'll also have the option to display a profile photo, which is recommended as the app is extremely visual. Matches are based on geographic targeting and its interface allows users to see when others are online and how close they are. You'll be able to see all the available profiles within a specific area. If you see a photo that rocks your world, by "Tapping" on it you will see his full photo, information and how far away fun is for you. You can save users as "Your Favorites" by Tapping on "The Star", and his profile will continue to appear with a "Yellow Dot". "The Green Dot" indicates a user is online. If you don't want a profile to appear again you can also choose to block that user.

The "Orange Toolbar" displays five icons used for various functions.

The "Mask Icon" at the very left contains the main menu to view and edit your profile, to change settings, help button, and subscribe to "Grindr Xtra".

The "Speech Bubble" is all your chats, and when you have new messages.

The "Circle" hides offline users and shows those who are currently online.

The "Star" shows users you've added to your favorites.

The "Three Rectangles" sets your filter options.

The best feature about Grindr is the "Send Location" feature which allows you to see exactly where and how close a user, that is currently online, is to you. My friends that use this app say if they want to get laid at 9PM they will go out at 8PM, use the app to find the person and be done by 10PM.

When it's time to spend money for a boost when messaging, use "Gaymoji", If you want to get the most out of the app, pay for the premium feature, Grindr Xtra. Members get the following features: Ad-free experience, view over six hundred profiles at one time, get additional photo filters, unlimited blocks and favorites, save & send chat phrases, "Quick Send" recent photos and Grindr Tribes.

This app improves gay men's dating lives considerably as an app that comes to life whenever you literally "want it". Millions of users log on daily to use this app looking for a hookup, also don't forget to sync your social media to your profile. Remember to have a face picture as well for your profile. Also add a variety of pictures and make one a full body shot. Don't give the impression that you are hiding something if you give five face shots. This is huge on Grindr. Tapping is a huge practice on this app and should be your number one action. Finally avoid the deep shit. It's a turnoff. Keep it light not the kind of website. Get the conversation off Grindr as soon as possible. Try and get it to Snapchat or Instagram. Know what you want before you start using Grindr. If you are looking for a hookup, make that a goal. If you want to date be up front with people. Don't have half-ass conversations with someone that will mix you up.

CHAPTER TWENTY-ONE

YOU GOT TO HAVE FAITH?

Christian Mingle is the leading Christian dating site for single men and women looking for a relationship centered around God. Jdate is the largest Jewish dating site for singles in the world. I took the two most popular religious dating sites in the world and I wanted to see how they do it. First, I will look at the reviews for both sites, any pertinent info or statistics that stand out and then I will set up profiles for both sites. In the end we will compare both.

First up Christian Mingle verbatim reviews. Karen of Miami on Yelp gave one star out of five and said:

"For a $49.99 a month I think the owners of this site should really check the subscribers. In fact, I don't think the fake accounts are from outside I think it is in house. A way to cause you to renew the subscription. Everyone that contacted me were fake accounts. This site is corruption and fake please don't waste your money. Don't deserve any stars but I have to click something in order to move on."

Second is verbatim review Laura of Val Alstyne, TX on Yelp gave one star out of five and said:

I joined Christian Mingle 3 days ago! I signed up for the three-month subscription and thought that would give me time to search and hopefully meet some interesting people. First, I live near a large urban area, but when I searched within 100 miles there were no matches available. My search criteria were open, and it had to be extended to 500+ miles to get any matches. At that point I started getting the "Smiles" and a few messages. I did respond to one message and we started texting. It was a good conversation. I fell for the "my subscription is going to expire can I have your number?" At that point the whole feel and tone of the writing changed. First red flag was when he started asking questions that we discussed earlier. Second red flag was when he sent pictures and it was a different person than the profile picture! He asked for my pictures, and if he was the person on the profile page, he would have seen my pictures.

Last is verbatim review Cathy of Big Sky, MT on Yelp gave one star out of five and said:

Although I am not a highly technologically savvy individual and may not understand how this seems to be happening more and more in the world of dating sites, I was absolutely astonished at my experience with Christian Mingle. I signed up and created my profile and within 4 days I had received over 100 contacts and emails, unfortunately not even one was legitimate. People, please be wary of the emails coming in stating such things as, my brother or my father or my friend saw your profile but does not want to join the site but he is a wonderful man and it would benefit you to contact him at (text or email).

Ok so if we sum up all three reviews, we will see that the people were not happy. These people felt threatened, violated, and ripped off. Some catfishing going on. Plus, these people were disappointed. Clearly these are religious people and they really took it personally.

First up Jdate verbatim review Jann M of Cedarville on Yelp gave one out of five stars and said:

> For years, I participated on Jdate until now. Jdate allows and promotes known felonists conmen and abusive customers to remain on their site even after being warned, given police reports etc.
> All for the money they don't consider the victims of these con men on their sites. Poor rating Has gone downhill last 4 years!!! Don't join! Terrible! I reported felon who currently is on their site. He is a con man wanted by the FBI and LAPD. And Jdate took me off their site not him! The worst! Bad Bad Bad! Con man nic borjas still on the sight Felon wanted Bad Jdate very poor Jdate is awful.

Second is Wendy G. of Mooresville, NC on Yelp gave one star out of five and said:

> This is the worst dating site. I was scammed twice and so fortunate to know what catfishing is all about. I thought I truly met someone special until, yup, the money question came up. I was finally out after the fifth attempt by someone to scam me. I reported each occasion and each account was deleted but no response to me nor any compensation, I wasn't even contacted until it was time to renew my membership. What a rip-off. ladies beware. I would mark this a zero if I could.

Finally, is Nathan C of Alexandria, VA of Yelp gave one out of 5 stars and said:

> Their technology is substandard and never gets better. The app is pathetic! Try logging-in and you'll find it goes to the sign-up screen 99% of the time.

> That's right, members don't matter because the app is all about forcing you to sign-up when you're already signed-up. They know it happens, but don't care. Next, you'll find yourself forever changing your password because your password won't work shortly after you've set it. It's a JDATE technology problem. Third, their prices are outrageous. I didn't have the option of selecting zero stars, which is what this company deserves.

Ok so if we sum up all three reviews, we will see that the people were not happy. These people felt threatened, violated, and ripped off. Some catfishing going on. Plus, these people were disappointed. Clearly these are religious people and they really took it personally.

Now let's just look at Christian Mingle's pertinent info and statistics that stand out. Been in business nineteen years. In 2019 Spark Networks, which owns Christian Mingle and Jdate, announced the acquisition of Zoosk. This purchase will double the amount of paying subscribers and makes them not only the second largest dating platform, but the second largest publicly listed dating company in the world. So, dating sites like Christian Mingle have the financial backing and the tenure to succeed. Jdate established in 1997 is in the same situation. So, if Spark Networks provides everything a dating site needs to succeed why is it getting such shitty reviews? Elite Singles even falls under this umbrella but is doing well. Zoosk falls under this umbrella but is doing well. Both have solid reputations with their clients. But when it comes to Christian Mingle and Jdate most of their clients can't stand them.

Now I am going to join Christian Mingle. First off you don't have to be Christian to do this site. You are seeking Christian men or women. They do offer men can look for men and women can look for women based on a lawsuit two years ago. Right away I gave a fake email and name. Basically, I was lying the whole time, because I did not want them having my information. I put in a fake picture of someone I used to work with and then I started listing my preferences. They asked me how many times I attend church. Then they tried to have me sign in with Facebook and I couldn't move on, so I had to join for real. So, I redo everything I just did and then I had to fill out a profile. I must have added the word God like five times. Then I put in all my interests. What am I looking for. Kid preferences. Relationship preferences. Then there was an "Advanced Features" which had my church schedule, would I relocate and my habits.

Next they offer me a membership and the features that come with it which are send and receive messages to paid members, hide your online status from people browsing your profile, anonymously check people's profiles which sounded really creepy and "Read Receipts" which is see and when people read your messages. How much is all this? 6 months at $24.99 a month, 3 months $39.99 a month and 1 month $49.99 a month. No thank you.

Now I was taken to the main page. Immediately I went to the upper right-hand corner to see my profile and add anything that needed attention. When I went to my profile, I realized it was only sixty five percent completed so I added more pictures and filled out my preferred first date. To the left is the "Activity Button" which shows who viewed me, I viewed, likes and mutual like. To the left of that is the "Matches Icon" which shows any matches I may have, and I didn't have any.

To the left of this is the "Messages Icon". Once I clicked under this there was a message from Christian Mingle that said:

At Christian Mingle we want to protect you in your online dating experience, and we need your help to do so. Please read and accept this important message. I promise to never send money, ask others for money, or share financial information with anyone I meet on Christian Mingle. In addition, I pledge to report anyone who asks me for money or my financial information.

They had me agree to this. Looks like this was and is still an issue on this website.

The last icon in the upper left is "Browse The Profiles". Each profile had a decent picture with their name, age, proximity, match percentage and the ability to heart them. Under this icon you could click the "Online Feature" which shows who is online currently. You could click the "Distance Feature" which shows who is closer. You can click under "Match%" for the best matchups via Christian Mingle. Finally, you can click under "Lookbook" which is where you can anonymously look at profiles one at a time and set your preferences.

Honestly Christian Mingle to me looks harmless. What probably gives it a bad reputation is the people catfishing and trying to extort money from people. It is pricey and based on what people said on the reviews I would think six times before signing up financially.

Now let's log on to Jdate. First off you don't have to be Jewish to join this site. When I joined through Facebook it is so much easier because my name, birthdate, gender, and email is already there. Next, I get to upload up to six pictures. Then the basic questions of height, have kids, want kids, occupation, which college and religion. The religious choices are other, willing to convert, Conservadox, Conservative, Hasidic, Modern Orthodox, Orthodox (Baal Teshuva), Orthodux (Frum), Reconstructionist, Reform, and Traditional. I chose other. As I continued to fill out the profile, I realized it was almost identical to Christian Mingle. Then I realized they were both owned by the same company I realized it is the same thing I just filled out on Christian Mingle. The only difference is they asked my synagogue attendance and if I am Kosher and I wrote not Kosher.

Just like Christian Mingle they ask me if I wanted to upgrade my account and get the features which are the same exact as Christian Mingle. The prices were a little more expensive 6 months was $29.99 a month, 3 months was $44.99 a month and 1 month was $59.99 a month. They wouldn't let me log out, so I resigned in. When I logged in the main page is the exact same as Christian Mingle. So, the only thing I did is fix my profile and fill in what is needed.

But after looking at both sites and filling out profiles they were almost identical and easy. I did get some hits, but honestly, I didn't act on them. I am not a very deep religious guy, but I was curious to see what was out there. I have dated both very religious Christian women and Jewish women as well in my life. But for settling down not on my Grocery List and there are way too many dealbreakers going on. It is disturbing knowing that all the catfishing and extorting that happened on these sites. It happens on most sites, but it seems to be a practice on these. My advice be extremely hesitant joining these sites. Put your faith somewhere else.

CHAPTER TWENTY-TWO

YOU DOWN WITH OAP?

There are people out there who may have lost a loved one, got a divorce, maybe haven't even found the love of their life yet or may even just want some company. These people need their own special dating site as well. We may call them senior citizens. But the dating world calls them "Silver Singles" and they need love too. Our Time is a dating site that caters to singles over fifty. It has a large user base with eight million user hits a month worldwide and the app is available on iOS and Android. The downside to this site is most features require a paid subscription and there is no identity verification process. Can everything we talked about like corruption, catfishing, extortion, and anything demeaning happen on sites like this? Absolutely and the sad thing is they do. Now most of these people are lonely and are looking for company. There is a vulnerability factor here and it may seem easier to con this clientele that either has money or is on a fixed income.

OurTime.com is a dating site released by People Media in 2011. The website provides the opportunity to interact and meet with other people in their area and even further. Users can search for pen-pals, friends, dates, long term relationships and even marriage partners. Now going along this line anyone over the age of eighteen can sign up for this site. If there is an issue lie about your age, because there is no verification for this. I may be looking for a cougar, which is an older attractive woman who may have money. The most common problem is that because of the site's target group; there are a lot of scammers creating fake profiles which take advantage of the site's users leading to most of them trying to steal money from them. Advice never send money to anybody they meet on the site.

When you sign up users fill out their preference, age and city they live in. There is an Our Time female coach there asking you questions like you won't understand anything. It is kind of insulting. Registration takes three minutes and you can put up to thirty pictures up at once which most dating profiles don't offer.

The website's layout is neat, easy, and organized. There are not many new features, it provides a chance for its members to use the site even while lying down or reclined on a chair. So, the free services are you can register an account, create a profile with a bio, list all your interests as well as preferences and you match search as many profiles as you would like.

The features on Our Time are very accessible and only available to paying members.

"Connectme" allows a client to safely and anonymously start talking to your match without giving out any contact information. How you make a call is click the "Connectme Button" on you match profile page to send a request. Once they accept your request to call a phone number is generated that both parties can use. You can answer the call, send a text and check your voicemail. You can also remove a connection by pressing the "X Button".

"Notifyme" is a paid feature that sends a notification to you when someone becomes available on the site that meets your specific guidelines.

"Matchme" is a feature that provides ten fresh picks for you that match you, so you don't have to peruse more profiles.

"Promoteme" is another paid feature where for sixty minutes your profile gets a boost and it appears at the top of all the profiles.

"Updates" on the home page allows you to see new things people are posting right away on the home page. It is a community type of environment.

"Message Suggestions" are given to people that have trouble starting a conversation. On your profile it will allow you to create four questions that possible matches can answer.

"Search Feature" allows you to swipe through dating profiles very efficiently.

The prices are $29.99 for one month, 6-month standard plan is $88.94 or the 6-month best value package at $107.94 which allows you to highlight your profile to give you more traffic.

Finally, "Flirts" are used as a form of expression when you have nothing to say but you want someone to know you are interested in them. "Profilepro" can help here. However, if you're not well-versed in expressing yourself, you can use the service. A group of professional writers will get the necessary information for you and finish your profile on your behalf, with the intention of making it look interesting and unique.

But OurTime.com does create a safe environment for older people to talk. Just like every dating site there is a chance of malicious people to show up. As long as they are careful connections can be made here just like anywhere else.

CHAPTER TWENTY-THREE

THE WATER COOLER

Every dating website/app out there have the same goal and that is to meet somebody. Whether they encourage chatting, sending a wink, a flirt, a message, a like or even a phone call it is done in a specific environment with a specific style. No style is wrong or right. You must see what works for you and of course know what you want. There are so many sites and apps out there that it will never end. I have covered the top, most popular and interesting dating sites/apps out there. But there are some that are worth mentioning. Some of them may be out there and some of them you just may not know exist. The following dating site/apps, in no particular order, are selections you should check out and be aware of.

AdultFriendFinder.com is strictly an adult site that happens fast. Where if you know any of the members you be discreet and keep the info to yourself. It takes one minute to sign up. You need to leave your email and create a username which for me took forever to come up with. Then you are in. Pretty much you stare at women or men, depending on your taste, in their bedrooms, shower or whatever activity they are doing. There are emails that come in with offers. It is a fun voyeuristic site. The desk top version is better.

FirstMet.com is a serious dating website that has over thirty million viewers from around the globe. The site is for branded mostly thirty-five to fifty-year-old people. More recently the site has opened to friendships and casual dating. The sign-up process is straight forward. There aren't a lot of questions that most sites bombard you with.

WhoChat is a dating app where you stay anonymous or not. It is your choice. It is a free dating app with very little to do for signing up. It connects you with nearby people. You will start chatting with no pictures or names until you decide to show them your picture. And the best thing is that you can choose to chat with a man or a woman. It is the best speed dating app ever. Download and install WhoChat on your smartphone or tablet.

Hily is a dating app that is free to a point but uses boosts that will cost money and is very similar to "Tinderplus" and "BumbleBoost". It works by using matchmaking algorithms which are based on machine learning, instead of location and attractiveness, which is what Tinder uses. Mostly a hookup app. The more the person uses the app with photos sent, mutual likes and how much you communicate, the more of a chance you can make better matches. Users don't get an attractiveness score but a risk score which is based on complaints, dialogue, and activity. Hily uses verification via Facebook and it does private live events like Match does.

Badoo.com is a dating site that is honest. Badoo provides an environment that is real with authentic conversation. They have strict usage guidelines; they don't tolerate inappropriate behavior and has a list of safety features, so you have a great dating experience. They have over four hundred fifty million users. They say be clear on what you are looking for in either finding a partner, chatting with people, or just making friends. They do offer a video chat feature.

BeNaughty.com is an adult dating site where they are looking for a partner for the night and not anything serious. Very simple registration and they ask you to be verified by email, but not many people leave their picture or any information on their profile. Only available for Android. This app works basically from your location. With a free account you can send messages, winks, see who viewed you, but that is only for women. Men must pay for all those services.

OneNightfriend.com avoid at all costs. The site is completely not trustworthy, and it is filled with bots sending fake messages. Users have received fake messages sent to blank profiles. This app will crash your search every time when you are looking for dating sites and it always appears in the top ten dating site searches. Many of the profiles are fake and are used from other dating sites. Clients will receive targeted messages from profiles that reached their search criteria and they never clicked under their profile.

WooPlus.com is a dating site for larger people or people that prefer that type. WooPlus is also a community where curvy people are embraced, free to be themselves and enjoy meeting someone comfortably. "Curve Lovers" is the proper verbiage used on this site. It is free and the sign up takes three minutes. You don't have to be curvy to sign up.

CampusFlirts.com is a dating site for college kids. But to be in the game you must have a valid college email to join this site.

Alumni can continue using Campus Flirts after graduation, but most of the members are college students interested in exploring the dating scene while enrolled in school.

SingleParentMeet.com is for all the single mom and single dads out there. Very family friendly community of online daters looking for both a buddy and companion. You have something in common with the people on here, because they either have kids themselves or don't mind dating someone who does. But you don't have to have a kid to sign up. Very high success rate and easy to sign up.

MyLovelyParent.com is where the children can invite their mothers and fathers to start dating again by creating a profile on their behalf. The kids get carte blanche and have the ability to write their parent's profile, check their inbox, put up pictures and send likes. Which gives the single mom or dad freedom to just have fun.

TeenDatingSite.com, also known as TDS, is a top online network for teens looking to put themselves out there. Letting their possible matches "From The Hot Or Not Game" know if they are a match or bouncing back to the photo-heavy dating profiles, Teen Dating Site provides a fun experience for high schoolers and college students seeking a friend or a date.

PinkSofa.com is a lesbian dating site. A dating network prioritizing in comfort, friendliness, privacy, authenticity, and social awareness. Solely based on searching locally, single women can meet one another and find solidarity in the lesbian community online. Many women who are curious are heavily involved in this site.

Swirl.com is an interracial dating site for singles of various ethnic backgrounds. A diverse dating network that allows you to set your preferences. It is free and sign up is easy, but if you want to make an impact and honestly meet people, they say pay the

$19.99 for one month and go out as much as you can that month. The selections are not as vast as a lot of repeat profiles keep showing up.

SugarDaddyMeet.com allows men to see a vast number of women looking for the finer life. Their tagline is, "Sugar makes life sweet.". The site allows a sugar daddy to meet millions of women and in turn allows the women to meet more adapted men. Any man can sign up but expect to spend money.

OutdoorDuo.com has members that can search through local profiles and join activity-based events like hiking, biking, sailing, or skiing. Outdoor Duo can introduce you to individuals seeking an active companion. It creates a friendly atmosphere. You can register as a member for free and start mingling in the niche community. The site prepares visitors with all they need to join a group of outdoor enthusiasts online.

SoulGeek.com allows nerdy people to talk, meet up and crash Comic-Con together. Forums, chat rooms, and blogs encourage a community feeling, so singles need not dive into private messaging right away. This is for singles who have a weakness for romance, but a huge intellect for smart fun.

SilverSingles.com is only for singles over fifty. It has a nice and clean website design and it's easy to use. You will fill out a personality test which is then used to find the best matching partners for you. It caters to mature men and women.

BlackPeopleMeet.com has become popular among black singles in America. The site gets around five million visitors per month so no matter if you're in a big or a smaller city, there should be a good amount of choices for you. It is the biggest dating site for black singles in the US.

FarmersOnly.com has a tagline that says, "City Folk just don't get it.". This is a website for good country folk that are very simple. Ranchers and farmers who want to meet down to earth people. Founded in 2005. It has millions of members and several weddings every week. They don't like city folk and a very tight knit group.

CHAPTER TWENTY-FOUR

THE FIRST IMPRESSION

The first date of any online date is the first impression and sometimes the only impression people get. It doesn't matter how many likes you sent or chats you had, when you see that person live and go on that date that is when decisions are made. So how do you properly prepare for that big moment? That is the burning question we need to answer. In order to do that you need to break it down into five parts. This helped me and many of the people that have helped contribute to this book. We came up with the blueprint that works and here are the five:

1. Be prepared.

2. Know where you are going.

3. Know what you are wearing.

4. Know what you are going to say.

5. Know if you want a second date.

Be prepared means know the history of the relationship. From the first minute of contact that was made between you two. How was it made? Was it a wink? Did you guys have something in common that inspired the conversation. Whatever it was things were said and it must be remembered, because these things will come up again in the conversation. Hopefully you built a foundation in your conversations that got you to that first date. Clearly you have things in common and you may want to explore more interests. So, before you even consider a date know their top three interests and incorporate that in your first date. What stands out about them? Why do you like them? Know these answers. Know why you want to spend time with them. How is the chemistry between you two and if it is good how do you keep that mix working? Remember the things that got you there.

When you are about to transition from online to offline, I recommend doing something relaxing before your date like listen to music, stretch, get a workout in or even call a close friend. This last part is two-fold. One you can get advice if you need it and two let someone know you are going on a date and where you are going for your own protection. Lastly clean your car especially if they are ever going to get in your car. On a first date have your own mode of transportation or if you don't meet the person there. But some people may feel there is a huge connection and may want to be picked up. Lastly make sure your place is clean. That includes your bathroom and while in the bathroom make sure you have protection if things go well.

Know where you are going means you know where the date is going to take place. This should a mutual agreement that results in both your interests and preferences. The most important thing to remember is to keep it casual, but interactive.

The following is a list of great places to go or things to do on a first date: a romantic walk, restaurant that can be a casual dinner, park, coffee shop, scenic car ride, comedy club, pub, live music, bowling or playing pool or a place with games and rides.

The following is a list of not great places or things to do on a first date: Theater or movie, cultural event like a concert, shopping, dance club, house party, yoga, a mixer, work party or wedding and even a sporting event.

Where you are going should be discussed in detail and the date should be two hours at most at that one place. It should be slow and paced out. Watch the drinking. Make sure it is not a place that will make you sweat or want to change clothes or make you feel uncomfortable. It should be one event where conversation is going back and forth. It should be a place where you can have a conversation and hear your date. Always offer places, especially places they would want to go. Make it about them. But remember something very important. If you recommend a place that is you asking that person out, then your date may expect you to pay. To be on the safe side always have your credit card ready just in case. Most people go Dutch these days for two reasons. They want people to know they can pay for their meal and they may be offended that you are paying for the meal or not. Again, watch the drinks. Honestly try not to drink. Your bill will be less expensive. Also, if you smoke don't that night. Keep your habits out of it for the night.

Again, know where you are going. If it is dinner, then you will know it is a two-hour thing where you can talk. If it is a park, make sure you have a blanket or a sweater for you and them if it gets cold. When you know where you are going you may have an idea when you want to leave before the night ends. Then three things can happen. One either you make fake plans like, I have to wake up early so you want them wanting more or two the date may be a disaster and now you have an out. Three you may want the date to continue and you do a mini activity like walk or get that first drink. Have that backup date plan ready to go.

Know what you are going to wear. That means dress the part and look your best. If you are going to dinner iron your clothes or even get your stuff dry cleaned. Make sure your underwear looks good just in case. If you are a guy, shower, pluck you nose hairs and eyebrows. Shave and comb your hair. If you're a woman shave your legs and wear some make up. What your wearing also means, how do you look? Things people look at. Guys trim your nails and make sure there is no dirt in them. Women notice this and think you are a mechanic. Wear a belt and tuck your shit in. Even if you have a belly don't look sloppy. First impression remember. Also, shoes are so important. Make sure they are or look new. If they are new, then you won't have a shoe smell. Put your phone on vibrate and away. That is what people look at. Also make sure you handle your money well and don't show an obnoxious wallet or purse even if you are paying. Ladies do not be a clocker with your heels. Men will feel like they are dating a horse. Now you are about to meet the person and the date is about to start.

Know what you are saying also means body language, how you say it, when you say it and when you don't say it. Watch your body language. Be relaxed. Sit appropriately. Get out of your head. Don't have any expectations of what you think they should look like. Give this person a chance. Don't exhaust all your conversation before you meet. Save it for the date. When you see them compliment them on what they are wearing or how they look.

When you open your mouth and talk make sure you spend the same amount of time listening. Make sure when you are eating that you chew and don't be sloppy with your food. Make sure you eat your meal as well. People get turned off when they don't eat a meal. Use the food and the environment to your advantage. When they talk make sure they have your full attention. Make sure you are nice to the staff helping you even if the service sucks. People see how you react around others.

Once you are settled and know you got the date flowing it's time to get down to business and take some chances. Remember chapter two The Grocery List and chapter three The Deal Breaker List, it's time to bust those out and go fishing. Know what you're going to say. You know what you want, can put up with and you put in the time to see this person. I may ask if they want to start a family one day. Where they plan on living? What they want to do usually tells where they want to live. Do they like kids and then want kids? If you are feeling a good vibe you can ask questions. It is your job to gather as much information as possible in a subtle fashion. You are on a mission. Now whatever your preferences are on meeting someone for a relationship or getting laid there is a certain way of approaching this. Eventually after some time and a certain point of the night you will know if you want to see this person again.

Know if you want a second date. If you know you want a second date you will take the date one of two ways that we mentioned earlier. You will end the date with the bullshit back up plan that you have an early morning which shows responsibility and maybe keep them wanting more. Two you do the backup date prolong the night, ask some more questions, and maybe make a move. Now your date might find it offensive or even a turnoff that you are calling the date especially if the chemistry is working. Now if the date isn't working both parties will get the hint and call it a night. But if you get enough information from your date and they pique your interest you are going to want a second date and immediately you are going to work for that before the date comes to an end.

A second date means you want this person in your life a little bit more, you need more information and you want to explore these feelings you have for them some more. Or you may just want to have more fun with them. So, try and suggest a more intimate date like dinner at your place or there's. Or a two-part date where you do an activity and then maybe a Netflix night. But the date will be longer this time. If they need time to answer respect that and give it to them. But usually you get an answer right then and there. When you get that green light then it's time to make your move.

So now you have the answer to the question we were trying to answer earlier. How do you prepare to make that first impression? Be prepared. Know where you are going. Know what you are wearing. Know what you are going to say. Know if you want a second date. Follow that and you will get your second date.

CHAPTER TWENTY-FIVE

DUCKS IN A ROW

The second date always tells it all. You already made a first impression and now it is time to see if this person is worth anymore of your time. Now it's time to put all your ducks in a row by asking the right questions, gathering the right information and finally make the right decisions. Why is the second date the most crucial? Well you must make a second impression and the stakes are higher. Anyone can have a good first date or do something good once. Let me see you do it again. There are three things that you must make sure of before the second date is over.

1. You must make sure that you go through your Deal Breaker List and get all that information that you need to know.

2. Go through your Grocery List and see if that person has any attributes on that list that makes you want to be with that person more.

3. Be honest with yourself and ask yourself three questions. How do you see yourself? How do you see your partner? How does your partner see you? Then answer them all. You will have your answer in the end.

Now before we start answering these questions we must prepare for the sequel. The second date gives you a true sense of your partner's potential to love. You start to learn about your shared interests, ideas, and goals which are all the things that bring people together.

Date two deserves way more credit than we usually give it. Why? Second dates are when you get to show off your real personality. Frankly you aren't as nervous this time around and since a mutual interest has been established, you can show your true self. Just make sure that your first date preparation and manners don't disappear. Don't drink more, listen as much as you speak and dress right for the date. People can be on the fence after a first date and this can be your second chance. Especially if you feel an attraction toward them. Also wait for it to happen. You don't have to feel a spark right away on the first date. After some conversation it may happen for you. Second dates are fun! Sixty one percent of single guys and seventy percent of single women are more excited by a second date than by a first date, according to the Singles in America survey.

Body language is everything once again, but now more heightened. Stretch out your body more by looking more relaxed. Lot's more eye contact. Laugh more. Smile more. Agree with the person more. Small touches here and there matter. If you can and feel it, hold their hand for brief moments. When you have a chance to kiss, take it. Also elevate your conversation by saying you are having fun. Live in the now. Don't lose the momentum you are gaining. At this point weird questions may come up like, "Why are you single?" or "Where do you see yourself in five years?". The answer is be witty. Give funny answers. Don't stress it and keep it light. "Haven't met the right one. Or in five years Disneyland always wanted to go there.". They can be your answers. They will respect the answer by your attitude. If they don't, then you are getting some answers.

Guys you should plan the second date. Something not as formal and more fun this time. You already know each other so offer her a ride. The activity and the location should be different, so forget loud places, cinemas, because it is hard to concentrate on each other. Dinner with an activity going on, like songs or comedy, or dinner theater. Murder mystery. Always bring up great things that happened on the first date once again. Ladies same goes for you, compliment the guy. Let him make the plans, the time and place. See what this guy can bring to the table. When you see him, a hug or peck on the cheek is always good. Also, a golden rule for both never bring up the exes. There is a reason they are not there.

Ok now it is time to go through your Deal Breaker List. Remember this isn't a long list and it should take two dates to get your information. Remember some deal breakers could be negotiated or not that important to you after you meet someone. We do deal breakers first, because these are negative feelings in your life, and they weigh more than a Grocery List. As an example, let's look at mine from chapter three.

1. They must like kids.

2. They must want kids.

3. They must like dogs.

4. I wanted a Caucasian woman either Italian or Hispanic.

5. I wanted a Catholic Woman.

6. I didn't want a woman with kids. I didn't want to raise someone else's kids.

7. I didn't want someone who smokes.

8. I didn't want a materialistic woman who was all about money.

9. I didn't want someone who does drugs.

10. I didn't want someone who was divorced. To me that was damaged goods with luggage.

Now this is my list. Once again, no judgment. Everyone has their own preferences, and these are mine. Some time with in two dates I would mention kids. How do you feel about them? But I would be a little subtle about it, like my brother has the most beautiful little girl. If a woman likes kids, they will talk about them. Now you explore that. They like kids. Ok she passed my number 1. My next question is do you have kids? This will take care of two of my deal breakers right there. If she responds no, I don't have kids that eliminates number 6, I didn't want a woman with kids. Which then I could close it out with do you want kids? If she says yes then that takes care of number 2, they want to have kids. If she says no then that could be a deal breaker for me, but it needs to be explored. For example, I was dating a Vegan. That didn't bother me and wasn't a deal breaker. She didn't want to have kids and she was supposedly allergic to my dogs and she mentioned money a lot. Numbers 2,3 and 8. Three strikes and three red flags. I loved her but I didn't want to live that way. Now going back if my date said she has a kid, but it was from another marriage. Hold on that is number 6 and number 10. Two red flags, but again needs to be explored. Is that kid in her life all the time or is it joint custody? Is this ex in her life anymore? Things I would consider ignoring if I really cared about her. Religion isn't important to me, but number

5 would be nice. It depends on her religion and how adamant she was about it. Same goes for smoking and drugs. I have done both in the past, but how much does she do it? This can come up in casual conversation. But you don't make any decisions now or that night. You now have you answers for your deal breakers. Moving on.

Bust out that Grocery List and see if any of their attributes are on your list. Let's go back to chapter three and show my list.

1. Thirty-five-year-old woman that can have a kid.

2. Looks. Semi attractive OK. I would deal.

3. I would like to settle down soon as possible.

4. They must have a career and contribute.

5. Habits should be something I can deal with.

6. I want someone with minimal luggage. Pets and kids.

Now this my list with my preferences. The most important things I want in a partner. My intention is to get as many things off this list as possible. It's a wish list. Not all of them will come true, but it is nice if some of them do. Now I had two dates to get all this information that I wanted. This is the fun part. These are things you can ask. Just make sure it is in a subtle fashion. The reason you are hanging out with this person is, because you probably want the top three things on your list. Using my list as an example there is nothing wrong with wanting a kid and getting married to someone attractive. Most people want that, but you may be attracted to someone that is not as attractive as you expect. Here is where you must make some exceptions or change your way of thinking. Also, they may not want to get married, but have a kid.

So again, you may have to adjust that list a bit. Going down that list it is easy for me to ask what they do for a living and their profession may not be up to my standards. You may be embarrassed of your partner's profession. I am an actor and a waiter. I had women I dated look down on that. But after a while and at the end of the day you must be happy with yourself and not try to win everyone over. What kind of habits do they have? Do they drink, smoke, or do any kind of drugs? Can you handle their habits, because you don't want their habits becoming your habits? Last on my list is I want someone with minimal luggage. Good luck. Everyone has some form of luggage. Question is can I deal with it. No matter what Grocery List you have try your best to get as much info as possible so you can move on to the end and be honest with yourself.

Honesty can be brutal, but it's necessary to know. Do you want this person in your life once this date ends? Three questions you must answer is how do you see yourself? How do you see your partner? How does your partner see you? If you see yourself as someone who has a lot to offer and is ready to share your life with somebody, then you're ready. If you see your partner as someone who you could love and can be proud of then you're ready. If your partner sees you as someone, she can share her life with, love and be proud of and you can feel that then you are ready. The second date is the date that tells you what you need to know. What happens after that is life. You can have a great third, fourth and fifth date, but then never hear from them again. It happens. But if you did everything in your power to make that relationship happen then you can't beat yourself up. Time to start all over again.

CHAPTER TWENTY-SIX

THE HAMSTER WHEEL

No matter how many times you like someone, start a chat, go on a first date, make it to a second date and beyond there is that chance that you may have to start over again. Some people get discouraged at it while others see it as another adventure. It all depends on how you look at it. But after a while it can take its toll on you emotionally, mentally, and financially. The heart can only take so much and after a while it can feel empty. Your brain may need a fucking break from all the rejection that could build up or from crazy people you may have met. Of course, dating and these websites are not cheap and after a while you could have made some extra car payments instead of blowing it on strangers you considered a significant other at one time. So, what do you do when this time comes? Here are five suggestions:

1. Give yourself a thirty-day vacation from it.

2. Give your profile a complete make over.

3. Do things completely different.

4. Hit up five dating sites at once and engross yourself in it.

5. Give yourself a time limit for it then quit for good.

A vacation means time away from the life you were living every day. A break emotionally and mentally. Time to recover. Damage was done. Your mind was telling you things that you started to believe. Time for a clean slate. No matter what you did and no matter how many people saw your profile all that doesn't matter. You had some great times that you remember. You had some weird times with the people that you met. But now you are doing something else whether it's working out more, not drinking or simply watching porn. As long as it's not online dating. Get off social media for a month. I did it and it did wonders. I wasn't concerned about who likes my post or what other people were doing. I disappeared and as the days went on, I worried about it less. I calmed down and started to rethink things. I was getting my energy back and motivating myself to go back to it and give it another shot. Don't focus on the past, focus on the future. Whatever happened with an ex happened and it never needs to be discussed again. You got to be ready to move forward.

When you are back from vacation give your profile a complete makeover. This means new pictures you have never used before. Almost like you don't give a fuck. Use pictures that would make people think why would he use this? Your bio should be something short, opinionated, and completely different from what you wrote before. Time to attract a whole new crowd. If you were looking for a long-term relationship you aren't anymore. Now you are looking for fun and no labels. Really shake up the pot. Your interests really aren't your interests anymore. Put down Yoga. I hate Yoga but it worked for me. I met a whole new wave of people and I put up with Yoga, because I was having fun with the person I was dating at the time. Many dating sites like Hinge use fonts. I went off on a tangent when it came to those and it gave me traffic like you wouldn't believe. I took up smoking, marijuana, and drinking. I wanted to be a bad ass. It became more fun than the last time I did it. My ice breakers were more like ball breakers. It pissed certain people off and it started conversations with more people than I had before. I started paying for more of the services and it gave me more opportunities to showcase my new profile.

I did things completely different by doing the opposite to a point where I didn't give a shit what people thought, and I started getting responses. Talking to women like I didn't have time for them made them reach out to me. Some would try to correct me or even go out of their way to meet me. When it came to sending messages, I would comment on a profile picture saying what were you thinking making this your profile picture? They had to respond and three times out of ten I got a date. But eight out of ten I got a response. I wasn't bored anymore. I wasn't that hamster on the wheel. I was going somewhere. Video chats became my thing. I had women really open to me. But I got offline fast and met them in person. I was using online dating to my advantage and I was getting good at it. I would swipe threw all matches immediately and then search for more matches. When I was through with one site I jumped onto the next. I checked each site two times a day. Sometimes going through one hundred profile pictures daily.

Next, I was hitting up five different dating sites a day and paying top price for each one. First, I would hit up Tinder. I would swipe my daily matches and then I would try to set up any dates I could possibly get for that week. Dating was a form of working out and I had to stay in shape. Then I would head over to Hinge and look for something meaningful. There weren't a lot of selections, but they were nice selections to look at. Then I would go to Plenty of Fish and deal with lots of characters. I would get the occasional date, but really nothing to write about in this book. I met anyone from those sites for drinks. My fourth choice was eHarmony and I would meet nice people on that, but rarely did I get to a second date with most people. They were hardcore serious with high standards. Finally, and daily I would check out Coffee meets Bagel and there was always a nice match there. Couple of times we almost hit it off. I used two different emails for all the sites, and I was getting responses. I noticed my approach was all wrong when I first started. I was moving to slow. You just must jump in the water and move. I was really into it and I realized if I really wanted to meet someone, I was going to have to do it this way. Instead of treating every date like this could be my wife I had more of a freedom doing it this way. I was still holding onto my Grocery List and Deal Breaker List, but there were times where I just wanted to go on a date without any pressure of how it was going to go. I was really into it so much that I realized I was really learning about the online dating world, so I joined more sites and met more people. This gave me a great idea, why not share my knowledge with others and see if I can make some money out of it. Hence the idea for the book came about.

    I gave myself one year to check out all the sites and gather all the information I could. In that time, I did meet two different women from the real world that I dated. It was very hard to visit all the dating sites and write an online dating book when you are dating someone. So, I was delayed, but still on a mission. As I said earlier, I would give myself a time limit and then I would quit online dating for good. I have that date in mind, but I still have time to do some more exploring. You see I rediscovered a world in a whole new different way. There are certain strategies you can use for online dating. Just because one strategy doesn't work doesn't mean another one won't. I was a hamster on a wheel that felt I wasn't going anywhere and then with a slight adjustment I struck gold. So now I'm writing this book and sharing my knowledge for people who felt like me. Lost.

CHAPTER TWENTY-SEVEN

APPLES TO ORANGES

In this chapter Apples will be played by Online Dating. Oranges will be played by Real Life Dating. They are both in a diner having a conversation about who is better.

Apples: When I look for a date, I have more options than you!

Oranges: Yeah at least I know who I am "really" talking to.

Apples: You are just jealous, because most of the time I just pay to ask someone out.

Oranges: I don't have to pay anything to ask anyone out so why would I be jealous?

Apples: Jealous, because I pay up front and I am done. For you it is a nonstop cycle of paying from beginning of the date to the end. Sounds expensive.

Oranges: Well at least I don't extort money from people.

Apples: Well at least I can talk and date all types of people without anyone seeing us in public.

Oranges: Well at least I get fresh air.

Apples: Hey don't forget the date starts with me getting it going and then it moves on over to you.

Oranges: I don't need you to warm up the car. I can jump start it myself.

Apples: Sure, that is why you need me, because you don't know what to say to anybody.

Oranges: I don't need to write down everything I am going to say to people. I just say it.

Apples: Yeah and if you just wink, they might miss it. When I send it, it's a pretty big deal.

Oranges: At least I don't have to plaster my interests all over the place. I can just do my interest as my date.

Apples: Great way to limit yourself to just one thing.

Oranges: At least I don't use prompts in my everyday conversation.

Apples: Because you don't know how to properly use them!

Oranges: That is the thing no one uses them in everyday conversation. So why would it be OK now?

Apples: You know what you need? A good ice breaker.

Oranges: Oh yeah that is so much better than a prompt.

Apples: Hey do you folks still shake hands or are you still social distancing?

Oranges: Hey that's not cool!

Apples: What to soon?!

Oranges: Yeah well, I think it is kind of pathetic that two people do video chats in two separate rooms to try and make a connection.

Apples: Yeah it is so much better to stand six feet apart from one another wearing gloves and a face mask trying to hear what the other person is trying to say.

Oranges: Well do you have any better ideas?

Apples: Actually, no I don't.

There is a silence at diner table.

Oranges: Do you think things are going to change?

Apples: They already have.

Oranges: Any suggestions?

Apples: Maybe we can work together.

Oranges: Well we both kind of want the same thing.

Apples: Ok let's not stress out. How can we turn this around?

Oranges: Keep up the conversation you are good at that.

Apples: And get them out and about you are good at that.

Oranges: Yeah, I like that thing you did on Match.com with the live events.

Apples: Well I was thinking about you.

Oranges: It's not one way or the other.

Apples: It's both.

There is another silence at the table, but they are both smiling at each other.

Oranges: What now?

Apples: Well once this thing clears up it may be a while before people jump in the water again.

Oranges: But that will be the day won't it?

Apples: Yeah, a lot of winks and flirts coming your way.

Oranges: We do winks. Not flirts.

Apples: Why not?

Oranges: We just flirt. We don't send it. We do it.

Apples: Yeah but it is so much cooler when you send it.

Oranges: We send it. Just a different way.

Apples: Kind of like us huh?

Oranges: Yeah kind of like us.

CHAPTER TWENTY-EIGHT

COVID-19 DATING 101

Things are going to be different. This is an event that has changed our lives globally. A pandemic is defined as (a disease) prevalent over a whole country or the world. It has changed our economy, affected people's lives, the way they live and the way they act. And we don't know how long it will last. But it will change things and the way people deal with other people. It will affect the dating world as we know it. If you throw in the factors of people possibly catching the disease, the fear of catching the disease, social distancing, and the mentality of how people will act in public when it comes to touching, meeting somebody is not even in the conversation. So now we stay at home. But what will build is a longing. A longing of what it was like before it happened and that is something we cannot not ignore.

The weekend before all this happened, I ran my eighth consecutive Los Angeles Marathon on a Sunday. Everyone was out, but everyone was wearing gloves and staying away from each other. I saw it happening. So, the next day I called someone special from my past and I took her to the happiest place in the world Disneyland, because she had never been there before. I knew something was coming and I wanted to really enjoy it. I soaked in every moment of that day and it was one of the best days of my life. Two days later I decided to have drinks at a bar with a couple friends and that was the last social gathering I remember. Everything closed that weekend. I lost my job. I was told to stay home, and I couldn't really see any of my friends. People started buying all the toilet paper, food on the shelves and there was a panic. Things shutdown. How did this happen? It did.

That longing I was talking about earlier. It will build in people. People will want to be in bars and restaurants again. People want to go to the gym again. People want to go back to work again. People will go to salons again, because they want to look good again. People will want to date again. People still date online, but now it's only conversations and video chats. But it is the longing that will drive us to step out of that place we have been living every day for the past two months and go out and see people. A hug will mean more to people now. A kiss will mean more to people now. Sex will mean more to people now. A simple holding someone's hand will have a whole new meaning now. It will be deeper. It will mean something more. People will not take each other for granted anymore. People will get engaged more. People will get married more. People will want to start a family more. People will want to see their family more. People will celebrate more. People will date more. They will get that internet dating chip off their shoulder and take more chances. Not right away, but as time progresses and things start looking better you will see it in everybody. People will start getting their freedom back. Their spirit and their will to live and take more chances and live life. People will be inspired to try new things. People will be asking people out all over the place. It will be a glorious day and it will happen.

What's the lesson here? All you have to do is meet one person if that is all you want and then it's done. The search. All the work you put in. A new chapter begins in keeping that relationship. I have been talking about online dating the entire book and it is a beautiful and essential way to meet people in today's world. As you get older the window begins to close when you are trying to meet new people. Not in the internet dating world. There are endless opportunities here. Ever since the pandemic started, we have been moving further away from that and that must change. We must get internet dating back in our lives if we are going to enjoy that day. Like I was talking about earlier where everyone comes out again. I tell people get online and jump in the water. It's fun, scary and annoying all at the same time.

What I did for the people that just read this entire book was paint a picture for you. I was like Magellan the explorer who took you all over the 2020 dating world and I made a map for you. Now it's for you to decide where you want to go. A year from now when we get through this and look back on this, we will have a deeper appreciation for it all. What we went through and how we got through it.

But for now, its's Covid-19 Dating 101 which stresses more conversations in the dating apps and there has been a 25% spike increase in the United States. Dating apps like Hinge are adding a "Dating From Home Feature" that allows daters to have video chats. Also, they are deploying "Date Ready" is a feature where daters give their availability for phone sessions. Tinder is expanding "TinderU" for college students. So, when college students are stuck at their parent's house for the pandemic, they can match with their university colleagues remotely. Even more people have seen more advances toward each other through LinkedIn. Plenty of Fish rolled out live streaming functionality to encourage singles to date from a distance. People are even rekindling with people on Facebook. Remember that place where you left family members and friends you never see. Now is the time to talk with that ex if you want to. Skype videos may even make a comeback.

At the end of the day internet dating is not going anywhere and regular dating will make one of the biggest comebacks of all time. Touch is something we take for granted. It is a tremendous stress reliever and when you trust somebody it makes it better. I think once Covid-19 is all over dating won't be considered a job anymore, but a privilege.

EPILOGUE

There really is no book like it! Where you get to visit every relevant dating website/app out there. What each website/app represents and has to offer. How much they cost. The good and bad aspects of each site. The 2020 online dating situation updated for any curious user. I was overwhelmed when I first started. Online dating scared me and intimidated me. But I know I was missing out and I didn't want that to happen. So, I got up off that couch and I just dove in. I gathered information and I learned fast. I talked to other people in my boat who wanted to meet new people for their own reasons. But the goal was always the same. So, I shared our stories.

We looked at changing your way of thinking. How your needs and preferences were important, so you made a Grocery List and your Deal Breaker List. You were given different options on what dating sites worked for you. You now had options and you learned the pitfalls of online dating. Words like catfishing, extortion and ghosting are now a known thing. You know the fun dating sites and the ones to avoid. Filing out an online dating profile is now cake and you know what to write in your bio and what profile pictures to post. You are now a swipe master and sending likes and flirts is in your everyday regiment. You know what it takes to make a first impression on a date, and you know what to do on the second. If you ever get tired of online dating you know how to refresh and revisit that feeling. Covid-19 is a real thing that impacted millions of people around the globe and there is a process that we will go through to get back to a sense of normalcy. Of course, many aspects of life were affected by this. One is the dating world and people's attitude will change when it comes to dating. I believe people will embrace what they didn't have for a while. It will become a time when people will put other people first and change their ways in a more positive way.

As I mentioned, online dating is not a job. But a privilege. I now feel a freedom when I go online looking for adventure. There is an opportunity for me to meet someone that I never met before that can change my life forever. It only takes one and then I am done. No more profiles or online dating. That is when I quit like I mentioned I would. I did this book for myself. To prove that I did have something to say and I could share this knowledge with people. I hope this book taught, inspired, and entertained you. I thank you for getting it. Reading it. Hopefully you got something from it. I sure did. AGOOSH!

www.ingramcontent.com/pod-product-compliance
Lightning Source LLC
Chambersburg PA
CBHW060833050426
42453CB00008B/676